# THE CARTHUSIAN CONNECTION

## *The Trail from the Cathars to Shugborough*

# THE CARTHUSIAN CONNECTION

## *The Trail from the Cathars to Shugborough*

*Maxwell N Field*

Fivepin Limited, 92 Crane Street, Salisbury, Wiltshire, SP1 2PU
www.fivepin.co.uk

British Library Cataloguing in Publication Data
A catalogue record for this book is available from the British Library

©Fivepin 2006
ISBN: 1 9038 7741 5

Printed in the UK by Lightning Source, Milton Keynes

# ACKNOWLEDGEMENTS

Because of my longstanding friendship with a particular French friend, I have been able to visit and walk not only the area in question but also far and wide in Savoy and Isère over the last twenty-five years.

My thanks, therefore, go firstly to:

*Aimé Faucher*, a native of the Maurienne and Chambéry region, a former pupil of and then a geography/history teacher at the Lycée Vaugelas in Chambéry, former President of the Savoy Rugby Federation and a stalwart of Chambéry Rugby. He is also co-author and researcher of the first ever book on the whole history of Savoy rugby over the last 100 years – a massive undertaking. I also gratefully recognise the valiant help provided by his wife, *Odette*.

My wife, *Marine*, who has wondered what I was up to on many occasions, hunched over maps and spending hours delving into volumes on the distant history of the Chartreuse. Her untutored eye in these areas of research has been instrumental in filling out the explanations of many aspects of the book, so that my assumptions about what readers might already know on the subject do not leave too many gaps for them to fill. Her native French, rather than my learnt variety, has been invaluable in checking my draft of the French version of the first section of this work, along with my sister-in-law, *Marie-Aude Lambert,* and a family friend, *Diane Ratel*.

# Acknowledgements

Also in France:

**Roger Piet**, a financial consultant and also a previous long-standing servant of Chambéry Rugby Club. Roger and his wife, **Monique**, have helped me get to some, literally, dizzying heights over the years deep in Savoy.

**Yves Cérino**, of the Antiquarian Bookshop, rue de Boigne, Chambéry, for his unstinting help in unearthing valuable connections for my local research.

**Father Soldo**, of the Maison Diocésaine of Chambéry, for his helpful advice on reading the first section of the research and his provision of volumes on the Carthusians.

**Marcel Jay**, a well-respected guide of the Association of the Heritage of Savoy, for his patient appraisal of the first part of my research.

**M. and Mme Bonaz** of Sonnaz and to **M. and Mme Trépier and family** of Aillon-le-Jeune for welcoming a complete stranger into their households at a moment's notice to talk about local history, thereby helping enormously with important details.

**M.Ortolland** of St Jeoire who took time to give me a personal tour of its priory and **M.Terreaux** who was eager to impart information over the phone.

**Mme Etallaz** of Pragondran for welcoming me into her home and for her unstinting help at the Town Hall at Vérel-Pragondran.

**Monique, M.le Maire – M.Dumaz – and his staff** at the Town Hall of Les Déserts for their help while under considerable pressure from other callers.

**The staff** of the History/Religion Sections at the Médiathèque J-J.Rousseau and at the Archives

Départementales in Chambéry, who have diligently sought various documents and books in answer to my very localised questions.

**Mme Laurence Sadoux-Troncy** of the Documentation Service of the Musée Savoisien in Chambéry for her outstanding efficiency in finding information on the etymology of local site-names.

**M. André Palluel-Guillard**, Honorary Professor of History at the University of Savoy, through whose efforts I was able to find documents relating to the Carthusian emblem.

In England:

**John and Joy Millar**, who jointly run the **Saunière Society**, for providing me with the platform to recount my research at some of their prestigious symposiums at Conway Hall in London and at Newbattle Abbey, near Edinburgh.

**Henry Lincoln**, for his appreciative reception of my lectures and helpful comments, after providing me with the impetus all those years ago to conduct geometric research in Savoy along the lines he initiated in Rennes-le-Château.

**Greg Rigby**, whose published findings on alignments, the Great Bear and St Robert of Molesmes provided vital connections towards the progress of my own research.

**John Skermer** for his advice on my manuscript and his most helpful suggestions in finding the publisher for this book.

**Russell Gethings** of the Shugborough Administration Dept, for his guided mini-tour of the most important aspects of the estate and his help in finding more obscure background details of the perplexing issues.

# Acknowledgements

**Liz Stacey**, of the National Trust Photo Archive for her most efficient and friendly help in locating and providing visual historical details about Shugborough.

In Scotland:

**Dr Gordon Strachan**, lecturer at Edinburgh University, Church of Scotland Minister and well-respected author, for his unstinting support and encouragement for my research.

**Jean Greyling**, for welcoming me to her home in Edinburgh and providing me with more sparks of inspiration.

**Jim Munro**, for providing advice and in-depth knowledge about Rosslyn Chapel and the Templars.

**Joe Pauswinski** and **Ron McNees**, two American stalwarts of the Saunière Society for their supportive thoughts on interpreting data.

But mostly to **Aimé**, who scoured the French version of the first section with an eagle eye, who has accompanied me and driven me about on a myriad of walks of discovery, has guided me around his native Savoy for twenty-five years and who has acted as a down-to-earth sounding-board for my (outlandish) ideas in the best French schoolmaster tradition. He has been the stalwart friend for the whole of the time.

Opposite is Aimé on an afternoon when we were navigating the Fouda Blanc path in the Chartreuse. The steep grassy slopes along which the path runs are not recommended on windy or rainy days!

# The Carthusian Connection

# CONTENTS

# Contents

# Contents

# FOREWORD

The scope of research possible when confronted with such wide subjects as the Carthusians (les Chartreux), the Cistercians, the House of Savoy, the Templars, the Cathars, and Mary Magdalene is truly mind-boggling. Hence I have had to be very selective in both reading material and precise areas to be covered within those subjects. I have only had time to choose from those specific areas which I consider relevant to my somewhat different approach, which will probably be difficult to accept by some. Yet the whole does fit together, probably owing to the fact that I have had to use this 'skeletal' method.

If the select bibliography at the end seems rather short, it is because I have itemised the many books and authors within the text as I have proceeded. Endless footnotes do become very wearing and break up the eye's concentration, when trying to follow the text. When racing against time to scour books and documents in French places of reference, notably Archives, before having to return them at regular short intervals to get at the following batch, it has often been my mistake not to note them all down. There have been very many works consulted which are not, perhaps erroneously, mentioned in the text or in the select bibliography at the end.

Where translations of French texts have been required, I hope my renderings do not seem stilted. I have tried not to stray too far from the actual French to give the meaning.

Constraints of time and opportunity to visit Savoy and Burgundy before being able to walk up to many of the sites involved, combined with the contrariness of Alpine weather and visibility, have not helped me to take photographs of a professional standard. I hope, nonetheless, they convey the information with reasonable clarity.

Although the text is not very long, I think that it is detailed enough to warrant more time to peruse than would be initially considered necessary from a cursory appraisal. To help clarification, I have included a larger number of photographs and diagrams than might be considered normal.

I never thought, about ten years ago, that a chance observation from well-worn paths around Chambéry would take me on this 'journey' of discovery and unearth so much. Yet the time and effort expended have been well worth it . . . but I know there is more to do!

Maxwell N Field
November 2005

# INTRODUCTION

As aspects of the subject matter might well be unfamiliar to
English readers, I have tried here to give a brief indication
of a few areas referred to later in the book: Savoy (and Isère)/
Chambéry; the Bauges and Chartreuse National Parks; the
House of Savoy; and the Cathars.

To many people, **Savoy** [figure 1], in south-east France,
means ski resorts and **Chambéry**, a place you pass (or race)
through on your way to them! Courchevel, les Trois Vallées,

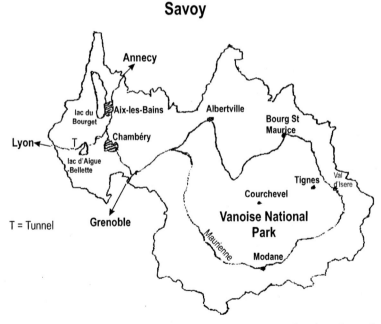

**Figure 1: An overview of Savoy. Geneva is to the north and
Grenoble to the south. The eastern frontier is adjoining
Italy across the high Alps.**

# Introduction

les Arcs, Tignes, Val d'Isère, the Vanoise National Park are well-known destinations further to the east and higher up in the mountains. But the major routes to them from Lyon and Paris pass through the Chambéry valley along the motorway or TGV rail network. Chambéry and Grenoble also provide an alternative and very scenic route down to the Côte d'Azure, via the Route Napoleon, thereby avoiding the motorway chaos usually encountered south of Valence.

## The Bauges and Chartreuse National Parks

**Figure 2: The two National Parks covered in the research, with Chambéry sandwiched in between. Grenoble is actually in Isère.**

On skirting Chambéry eastward-bound, there are two National Parks, one on either side: the **Bauges** to the north and the **Chartreuse** to the south [figure 2]. These are the northern Pre-Alps, blocks of mountains (massifs), cut horizontally by valleys. The ones that concern the reader are:

- the Chartreuse, an elongated rectangular massif with fortress-like outer walls, lying between Grenoble and Chambéry;
- the Bauges, somewhat more circular, lying between Chambéry and lac d'Annecy, and flanked by Aix-les-Bains to the west and Albertville to the east.

The terrain is harsh but villages have eked out an existence over the centuries and are now helped by tourism, also in the summer.

To the east of both massifs is the wide Isère valley, stretching from Albertville in the north to Grenoble and then arcing to Valence in the south. This valley is known as la Combe de Savoie (north) and the Grésivaudan (south).

The Chartreuse is split across the middle by the boundary between Savoy and Isère, the latter encompassing Grenoble.

Chambéry is the ancient capital of Savoy, just a dozen or so kms. south of the lac du Bourget, the largest natural lake in France. Just beyond the first tunnel back towards Lyon along the motorway is the lac d'Aiguebelette, a tranquil tourist-trap nestling up against the cliffs. The calm waters have hosted the World Rowing Championships.

Chambéry has existed as the capital for just over 700 years, so the history is immense and can be linked further back to the start of the House of Savoy family dynasty and the growth of monastic settlements in the area, among them being the Carthusians and the Cistercians, both of which are still on-going international Orders today. These ecclesiastical groups are described in more depth in the text.

In its fullest sense, Savoy is composed of the present-day departments of Savoie and Haute-Savoie and was historically strategically important for its mountain passes into Italy. Haute-Savoie is the northern section bordering lake Geneva and Switzerland.

# Introduction

The **House of Savoy**, since its inception in 1034, held control of this independent area which saw its borders periodically extended and then reduced over the centuries before it became part of France in 1860.

The rulers of the House of Savoy were Counts from the thirteenth to the fifteenth centuries and presided over a vast expansion of their territory, including Nice and Piedmont. In 1416, Savoy became a dukedom. Occupations and invasions by French (and even once, Spanish) troops at intervals caused the capital being transferred to Turin in 1563. Sardinia was acquired in 1718 and the dukes took the title of King of Sardinia which, in 1748, became the kingdom of Piedmont-Sardinia. Savoy was annexed by France during the Revolution but restored in 1815. Piedmont-Sardinia became the leading spirit in the movement for Italian unification and, after 1860, the House of Savoy ruled the newly-formed kingdom of Italy until 1946. It can be appreciated how complicated and, at times, devious the various alliances and political affiliations were to keep power over such a volatile area over such a long period of time.

The **Cathars** were a heretical Christian sect in medieval Europe. It is believed that they spread from Bulgaria, where its adherents were called Bogomils, to western Europe in the eleventh century. From the mid-twelfth century the Cathars flourished in southern France, notably in the Languedoc-Roussillon region bordering Spain, a prosperous and fertile area, and (mainly north) Italy. They were influenced by Gnosticism and Manichaeism, in that existence was ruled by a dualist idea: the material world was irredeemably evil, while the spiritual side and the soul were good and thus could secure reunion with God. They were very sceptical about much Biblical doctrine. They were a peaceable sect, with parity between the sexes. They were divided into two classes, the Parfaits (Perfects) and the Believers.

They were exterminated by the Catholic Church, in league with the king, by a crusade led by northern knights. The potent mix of anti-heretical fervour, greed for land, and envy culminated in the Albigensian Crusade (named after Albi, in the Languedoc) which began in 1208, led by the infamous Simon de Montford. The Inquisition joined forces with them in 1233. The genocide reached its climax with the taking of the last major stronghold of Montségur in 1244, when 200 sect members were burned alive at the stake at the foot of the hill. Isolated groups of Cathars held out in increasingly scattered areas for decades, for example in north Italy, but they were eventually hunted down.

Over the last few decades, a resurgence of interest in this historical domain has been led by French historians, both local and national. The Cathar strongholds, though not necessarily built by them, attract great numbers of tourists to the region. Ranging from almost complete ruins to vertiginous castle forts and the preserved splendour of Carcassonne, the powerful drama can still be sensed today.

# SECTION ONE

# PART ONE: THE CHAMBERY VALLEY AND MYANS

## Background and first alignments leading to Myans

'What a fantastic panorama!' has always been my silent impression when I arrive in front of the chapel on top of Mt St Michel, a smaller mountain among those that line the valley about six km to the south-east from the Savoy capital of Chambéry. The view plunges away at my feet straight down to Challes-les-Eaux and spreads out in a fan-like 180° arc from Mt Nivolet (which dominates Chambéry) to the Roche du Guet (which dominates Montmélian and the Isère valley).

In fact, it is this uninterrupted panorama which gives this summit an importance beyond its relatively un-remarkable height. Mt St Michel occupies a slightly more southerly position than its neighbouring mountains on the southern limit of the Bauges Massif and therefore nothing obstructs its view towards the Chartreuse on the opposite side of the Chambéry valley (the 'Cluse de Chambéry').

I gradually realised that some of these southern peaks of the Bauges, the Chambéry valley and the Chartreuse were closely linked in a system of remarkable alignments. This discovery was then to lead me into the history of the very founding of the Carthusian Order by St Bruno in the Chartreuse in 1084.

Two of the first and major alignments that become at once apparent when walking in the southern Bauges are between them and the Chartreuse. When the climatic conditions allow good visibility, I have always been struck by the silhouette of the Dent de l'Ours rising up behind the Col du Granier as seen from Mt St Michel and that of

3

**Plate 1: Mt St Michel, seen from directly beneath in Challes-les-Eaux. The wooded slopes rise very steeply up behind the casino and gardens adjoining the spa. The chapel is perched on the top.**

Chamechaude seen from the foot of the fissure in the cliff-face of Mt Peney, when standing next to the prehistoric 'daubings' on the rock wall. The Dent de l'Ours and Chamechaude are deep within the Chartreuse but the effect is as if you are taking aim down a gun-sight.

The view from the higher Nivolet which dominates Chambéry itself to the south and the lac du Bourget to the west contains the major peaks of the Chartreuse, with Chamechaude rising up behind Mt Joigny. But it does not have the same impact for particular peaks as from the neighbouring lower summits.

The facts that Chamechaude would be of pivotal importance later on and that the Carthusian monastery was

4

**Plate 2: The gun-sight effect, seen from the chapel on Mt St Michel and looking towards the Chartreuse. In the middle, the cliff-face of Mt Granier and its col; in the distance, the outline of the Grand Som (on the left), and the Dent de l'Ours (the little spike). Behind these two summits is the Carthusian monastery.**

situated just behind the outline of the Dent de l'Ours/Grand Som were waiting to be drawn out of my subconscious!

## *Henry Lincoln*

I have been very interested in the findings of Henry Lincoln ever since his investigations, allied to those of Michael Baigent and Richard Leigh, into the area of Rennes-le-Chateau were published in the international best-seller *The Holy Blood and the Holy Grail* in 1982. According to his geometrical theories, the geographical lay-out of the mountains is closely linked to that of the churches in the vicinity. For the Templars (the principal builders of churches and castles), the five-pointed star, or pentagram, was a powerful symbol, according to a tradition going back centuries BC. They had therefore established a system to reproduce, in the countryside, the geometric figure of a

5

pentagram.[For a more detailed description of the meaning of the pentagram, see pages 24 to 26.] How the surveying techniques were achieved over large distances is astounding; obviously the historical and religious backgrounds of the area have combined to form this amazing riddle for researchers.

The idea began to form in my mind that there might be some similar process to discover in the Chambéry/Southern Bauges/Chartreuse areas, as the different massifs are self-contained and have very distinctive peaks. The religious history of the Chartreuse is well documented and the Chambéry valley was and is of paramount importance as a channel between the two massifs, and as a gateway to the higher Alps. The latter has its own religious history, apart from its tenancy of the Holy Shroud before its transfer to Turin Cathedral.

### Myans – A brief historical outline

There are some very famous religious sites in the Chambéry area, such as Lemenc and its crypt, overlooking the city centre but in the suburbs, and Hautecombe Abbey, the last resting-place of the dukes of Savoy, which is beautifully situated just above the shoreline of the Lac du Bourget, opposite Aix-les-Bains. There are obvious reasons why these two sites are where they are (I was to discover others later), but the other main religious sanctuary – Myans – is in the middle of the valley. What were the reasons for this particular site?

According to Albert Pachoud and his detailed book *Notre-Dame de Myans*, the church, whose origins date back probably to the first centuries of Christianity in south-east Gaul, is situated on the top of a wide hill of about 40 metres in height which is aligned north-south in the valley centre. This spur is the remains of an ancient moraine left over from the time when the whole valley was occupied by a glacier. The east, west and north approaches were the swampy lowlands where now the main transport links are maintained. It is therefore easy just to say that the highest

**Plate 3: The ruins of the old chapel on Mt St Michel. It lies in a sheltered spot just behind the summit and the present chapel.**

place was occupied by the church, but there is quite a large flat area on top of this spur, so the first builders had a quite wide choice of exact location.

The main reasons for this church's fame are twofold: firstly, the worship is dedicated to a Black Virgin; and secondly, the miraculous survival of the church happened with the calamitous collapse of the north-east face of Mt Granier in 1248 – when the debris stopped at the portals of the church after obliterating everything in its path in between, so saving the monks' lives who had taken refuge there [see plate 3]. Hence its elevated position lent credence to the belief that Black Virgins were often the seat of miracles. Pilgrimages are regularly held in the summer and early autumn.

Its first mention on a map dates from the twelfth century and it belonged to the Church in Grenoble until the end of the eighteenth, when the Diocese of Chambéry was created. The cleric responsible for the setting-down on paper of the outlying churches under Grenoble's control was St Hugues who was later to figure largely in my investigations. It was he who helped install St Bruno in the Chartreuse and to found the Carthusian Order in 1084. Between 1080 and 1132 he showed himself to be not only a man of great faith, but also an excellent administrator. He wanted to find out how important each parish was that depended on his ministry as well as what they owed him financially. So he made up a list and mapped them, hence 'Ecclesia Meianes', the church at Myans, appeared on a map for the first time, along with others now disappeared under the collapsed debris of 1248. However, further afield in the valley there were marked Apremont, Chignin, St Jeoire and Murs (Les Marches). One was to figure again.

### *Hidden angles on a different viewpoint*

As you approach Myans from the west, Mt Margeriaz, whose peak is the furthest removed in the Bauges to the north, just slips out of view behind Mt St Michel. This fact always struck me, but its significance came a bit later. So the focus of attention is on Mt St Michel. As the eye sweeps round to the north-west, Mt Peney and Mt Nivolet are proudly displayed. It suddenly occurred to me that they are very evenly spread across the panorama, and the possibility that the church at Myans might have been sited exactly where it is, partly because of this, became enticing. The summits of Mt Nivolet and Mt St Michel are adorned with a cross and a chapel respectively (although the latter is about 100m. in front of the actual summit, but close enough not to make any real difference), whereas Mt Peney has no obvious summital point as the elongated wooded ridge is fairly even. Yet what catches the eye is the fissure roughly half-way along its cliff-face. This would seem to be the real focal point of the mountain, so I took this point as my reference.

I tested my idea on the map and found that the angle between Myans/Mt St Michel and Myans/Mt Peney was the *same* as that between the latter and Myans/Mt Nivolet – 12°. Could this be pure coincidence? If not, why should the mountains need to appear equi-spaced in front of it,

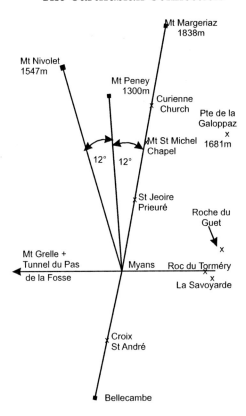

**Figure 3: The two major alignments in the Chambéry valley: north-south between Mt Margeriaz and Bellecombe; east-west between le Roc de Torméry and Mt Grelle. The two equal angles of 12° between Myans and the three mountains opposite: Mt Nivolet, Mt Peney and Mt St Michel.**

although the actual distance increases, the further north-west you look? If mountains have always been revered and were considered to have a beneficial influence over the places beneath, or even needed to be 'placated' in previous ages, then to site a church 'equally' before them makes sense. Almost every accessible summit is marked by a cross – a sort of divine place where Heaven and Earth 'met' and where gods convened – and so the tradition lives on with peaks dominated by the Christian symbol. Why should it seem odd or unnatural to want some measure of protection from the dominant physical surroundings? This configuration was surely not pure chance.

If there is a reason for this site when facing the north, then it was reasonable to assume that there could be another alignment from west to east. On drawing this line, I was again excited to see that it passed to the west through the sort of cleft in the spur of descending mountain towards Apremont/St Baldoph that is now used by the Tunnel du Pas de la Fosse. This hollow is now the route for electricity pylons, and is a natural feature visible from Myans. Further west the line reaches Mt Grelle situated on the Montagne de l'Epine – the southernmost spur of the Jura. Beyond Mt Grelle the land quickly flattens out towards the plain to Lyon. Mt Grelle appears as nothing spectacular from the east; only when viewed from the north does it become far more imposing as it rises above the rest of the ridge. Its wooded elongated summit is however of some importance, as shall be seen later.

To the east the line quickly terminates at la Savoyarde, or more particularly between that and le Tapin, which along with the aptly named la Roche du Guet, form the rocky promontory which commands a breathtaking view of the Isère valley between Alberville and Grenoble. This is the south-easternmost tip of the Bauges – another key feature. Again, could this be another coincidence, namely two important summits at each end of the line along the valley?

### *The big alignment*

My thoughts then returned to the fact that Mt Margeriaz dipped behind Mt St Michel when Myans was reached from the west. They were obviously therefore in line. Could there be anything further to this? [See figure 3.]

Reference to the map showed that from Mt Margeriaz to Mt St Michel, the line passes through the church at Curienne. At the present, trees obstruct the view from Curienne church to Mt Margeriaz, but it is certainly clear enough when the line of sight is restored by moving above the level of the church or along the road. However, in the opposite direction, the chapel on Mt St Michel cannot be seen – only a wooded rounded ridge is visible from the church. I find it hard to believe in the pure chance that these three points are joined in a straight line.

From Mt St Michel it now became evident that.the spur leading down towards St Jeoire was orientated towards Myans. Was this another hint latent in the geography of the area? Seen from the side, the spur is very long and is impressive as it rises up from the road below leading through St Jeoire. Halfway along the ridge, the ONF (Office National des Forêts) has erected a cross – the Tête de Beurre – which unintentionally highlights the very same direction.

Along the same line stands the Priory of St Jeoire (George) – or rather just off the actual line. The original building which no longer exists was alongside the present one (to the west). It was founded by St Hugues de Grenoble in 1110 and was conferred to the Augustinian Order. There had been a parish church there previously, which was already dedicated to St George. In 1110, St George became the patron of the parish. This could well refer back to the time when St Hugues was establishing exactly what belonged to him in the area, including Myans. It is interesting to note that the canons also served the parish of Curienne, among others. The alignment discussed here returns with separate significance towards the end of my research.

St George might, at first, appear a rather obscure choice for a parish saint. One point to be borne in mind here for later possible relevance is that the Templars used the cross of St George as one of their emblems, particularly on their shields. This is because the most important saint to them, apart from the Virgin Mary, was St George. Dr Helen J.Nicholson, a Senior Lecturer in Medieval History at Cardiff University and a specialist in the medieval Military Orders, states as much in the text of her lecture to the Saunière Society on 4 October 2003. St George had been an active warrior who had suffered a dreadful martyrdom at the hands of the pagans. This faith was an obvious model for the Templars to follow, in that death was preferred to denial of Christ.

## Part One: The Chambery Valley and Myans

Depicted in the stained glass window is St Anthelme, a noted cleric of the area, who became, significantly, a Carthusian monk and then Prior of the Chartreuse in 1139. He has a church dedicated to him in the ruined Tours de Chignin nearby – another important site of alignment to come. He is said to have prayed at Myans in his youth.

Geographical and historical links between this area of the Cluse de Chambéry and the religious seat in the Chartreuse were certainly highlighting the possibility that my investigation would proceed to the latter.

### The Southern Extension

From Myans, the ground rises gradually along the same axis until it reaches Bellecombe in the north-east corner of the Chartreuse – or rather just below it. The alignment [see figure 3] reaches the ruined church and fort walls which again provide an astounding view of the Isère valley up towards Alberville and Mt Blanc beyond it. The ruins are on the upper lip of a fold or step in the landscape (which might be the eastern extremity of the glacial moraine) and, as seen

Plate 4: The Croix St André, rising up atop a hill formed by the debris from the collapse of Mt Granier. In the background, to the east, the snow-capped Belledonne chain.

from Myans, the possibility that this could be a ley-line was enticing. This idea was reinforced by the southern spur of Mt St Michel along the same axis. One other unwitting addition lent credence to this.

The collapse of Mt Granier left the area below in a state of chaos, with high mounds of rock and ridges of earth all over the bottom of the moraine. One such high point overlooks the lac de St André – now a tourist trap – and a huge cross has been erected here [see plate 4]. This reshaping of the landscape happened roughly one and a half centuries after St Hugues mapped the area, but by some freak chance, the cross now erected on this prominent point lies in the same axis between Mt Margeriaz and Bellecombe [see plate 5]! It is as if the line was being continually highlighted. In fact, there is a very slight curve to the full alignment between the extreme points: Mt Margeriaz and Bellecombe. This led me to seek out any research done on ley-lines locally in the Médiathèque, the modern media library, at Chambéry.

**Plate 5: The whole alignment, between Bellecombe and Mt Margeriaz in the distance; Myans and St Jeoire are in the valley; the small mountain in the middle is Mt St Michel.**

# Part One: The Chambery Valley and Myans

## *Ley-lines*

The only references to this idea were unearthed in the archives after much explanation, and were not quite what I was looking for, but nonetheless I thought they might have a bearing on my investigation.

They were treatises of the early 1990s by François Garczynski, based in Grenoble, who is an engineer dealing with all rural aspects of watercourses and forests. IIis ideas and research were based on the 'rayons cosmotelluriques' (universal ley-lines) of Hartmann and Curry which have effects both above and below ground.

The 'rayons Hartmann' are energy lines of an electromagnetic nature which form invisible walls both above and below ground, gently inclined towards the north-west and following two general directions: north-south and east-west Their width varies from 10 to 80 cm. and the distance between them varies from 50 cms to 2.5 m, although on average this becomes 2.5 m. between north-south lines and 2 m. between those in an east-west direction. Where they cross is often marked by the presence of various insects and animals, eg anthills, bee swarms and cat claw marks on trees. There would appear to be a carcinogenic effect on plants or small animals placed for a period of time on a crossing of the lines. They are unstable, with solar flares, earthquakes and moon phases all affecting them. The 'rayons Curry' – about 4 m. apart – cover the Hartmann network in a diagonal way.

This did not quite answer my questions, but I thought that there was a fair chance that these 'rayons telluriques' would follow a mountain spur or fold in the landscape in roughly the right north-south direction. So possibly they would follow my whole alignment, yet no clearly visible signs would be apparent.

However, Garczynski went on to comment on both Alfred Watkins and Guy Underwood whose original research in England led to the ley-line theory.

On Watkins, he explained that he made out tracks forming lines which crossed through churches, castles, archeological sites or other landmarks such as raised stones or tumuli. Watkins called them ley-lines because of the high incidence of villages involved whose names ended in 'ley', 'ly' or 'leigh'.

On Underwood, Garczynski explained that on visiting old churches and archeological sites, he detected water channels and energy lines under the ground not linked to water. The former determined the tracks of religious monuments, stones, ditches and buildings, while the latter marked out tracks defining paths and roads. For Underwood, Watkins' alignments followed underground lines influencing plantlife and perceived by animals, which builders used to divide up and mark out the land.

Garczynski extended their theories by bringing in a third system – that of the sacred Roman networks applied to European megaliths, Egyptian pyramidal theories and Romanesque churches as explained by Jacques Bonvin in his numerous books.

This was leading back into my own territory to some extent, but I still could not prove that any ley-line was involved here beyond the geographical evidence already explained. However, at least Jacques Bonvin would have a further input into the Black Virgin at Myans.

## A second opinion

At about this juncture I ventured to ask a well-respected local guide, belonging to the Association of Guides of the Heritage of Savoy, for his opinion on my enquiries. Marcel Jay and I met for an hour or so at the Maison de Tourisme in Challes-les-Eaux. He was surprised to see how the alignments fitted into the landscape, but could not, of course, go beyond reserving judgement. At least he did not reject my findings and stated that this was the first time he knew of the area being investigated in this way. He did say that any further 'enlightenment' would be welcomed by him. His interest and his refusal to reject my ideas bolstered my confidence.

## Myans and the Black Virgin

Black Virgins are identified with Mary Magdalene through their geographical situation and their pagan or Egyptian source. After the initial work by Ean Begg *The Cult of the Black Virgin*, Picknett and Price in their book, *The Templar Revelation,* conclude that the link between them is very positive. Begg found that not less than 50 sites dedicated to Mary Magdalene have chapels containing a Black Virgin. A map showing the situation of Black Virgin sites indicates their main concentration to be the region of Lyon/Vichy/Clermond-Ferrand, with a series of hills in the middle, the Monts de la Madeleine. There are strong concentrations in Provence and the eastern Pyrenees, precisely two areas intimately linked to the Magdalene tradition. Hence the link is established.

French literature links Black Virgins generally to the cult of pagan goddesses, rather than to Mary directly. Michel Armengaud, in *Orcival,* states that the Rhône Delta is certainly the cradle of the Black Virgin tradition, with two centres being possible: les Saintes-Maries-de-la-Mer with Sarah, who was black, and Marseilles, where the Gauls worshipped Artemis of Ephesus, and where the Romans introduced the cult of Isis. From the Rhône Valley, this tradition spread towards the Massif Central and Burgundy. From the Delta, it spread to Provence, Languedoc, then to the Pyrenees.

Sophie Cassagnes-Brouquet, in *Vierges Noires,* Rouergue, Rodez, echoes these thoughts, in that a census of 1550 shows the route via which, starting from the shores of the Mediterranean – Languedoc and Provence, the tradition spread along the Rhône Valley, then along the Saône as far as Alsace. This style of statue indicates that it would have come from the Mediterranean. The only real contender for its geographical source would be Marseille, a city of commerce and cultural contacts, before the tradition spread along trade routes.

Lynn Picknett, in *Mary Magdalene*, states that the Black Virgin/Madonna phenomenon coincided approximately with the upsurge of influence of the Knights Templar, in the mid to late thirteenth century. Even though the main body of 'ordinary' Templars would have followed the mainstream worship of the Virgin and Jesus, there existed an inner esoteric group whose sentiments leaned far more towards the Magdalene and John the Baptist

Moreover, Picknett highlights the fact that these statues depict a mother *and child*. As Mary Magdalene is portrayed by them, then the inference is that she bore Jesus a child, or more than one. The depiction is obviously of a black woman. This could well refer right back to Isis and then to Mary. A marriage between Jesus and Mary resulting in children would have been enough for the Church to want to suppress the truth, let alone a mixed-race marriage.

Although this phenomenon is more widespread in the Auvergne and southern regions of France, I was intrigued to discover, through Jacques Bonvin and his book *Vierges Noires – La réponse vient de la terre*, that apart from Myans, the Monastery at la Grande Chartreuse possesses a Black Virgin as well, one that was allegedly found in the Holy Land when St Louis made it a gift to the Monastery. Like the one at Murat, it is one of only two made out of olive wood. Another Black Virgin is at la Tronche, a suburb of Grenoble just north of the river and on the route probably taken by St Bruno up into the Chartreuse.

Bonvin maintains that the siting of this statuette marks a sacred spot, one that is special, where the rayons cosmo-telluriques produce an intensity of energy emanating from the ground and linked to bio-magnetic forces. The Black Virgin allows this energy to be 'felt' by men and many miracles are alleged to be produced by Black Virgins through them. The ancient Gauls had an intimate knowledge of these bio-magnetic forces, as well as the Celts and Druids, so the history of this spot at Myans could well have been developed through many epochs.

Where two lines of the rayons cross, especially where one or several underground water channels or fissures are contiguous, then harmful or pathogenic effects are created, including carcinogenic ones. This knowledge was used to help our ancestors to construct houses, and also to build a temple or church or even to erect a menhir or dolmen. In this way the spot was neutralised, in that a crypt was built to amplify the better energy present, in the case of churches. So the positive energy flowed via the Black Virgin.

Bonvin also brought into his arguments the Hermetic theory that sacred geometry on Earth reflected the Heavens. So he was able to find the geometric form of the Seal of Solomon [see figure 4] superimposed over an area of the Auvergne to represent the sacred networks passed down the ages from the Egyptians, to the Greeks, the Etruscans, the Romans, and so to the Gauls. The points represented sacred stones and other bio-magnetic points in the landscape. Geometry was again being used to pinpoint sacred places.

Another interesting point about the Seal of Solomon and Myans is that the Seal has a real function with regard to the sun and stars, in that it determines the axes of the solstices. Using it as on a compass, with two points showing north and

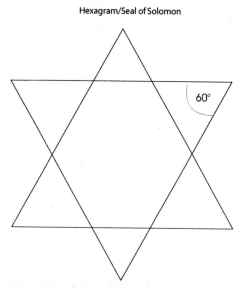

Figure 4: The Seal of Solomon (hexagram/six-sided star): each angle is 60°.

south, the 45° north-east point corresponds to sunrise at the summer solstice, the 135° south-east point indicates sunrise at the winter solstice, whereas the 225° south-west point gives sunset at the winter solstice, and the 315° north-west one positions the sun at the summer solstice sunset. This can vary slightly according to latitude, but by discovering the solstice axes, these orientations allow an observer to determine exactly the position of the statues of the Black Virgins and their sanctuaries. If they are correctly orientated in the churches, they face the north-east i.e. sunrise at the summer solstice. This is the symbol of the birth of sunlight and the light which will flood into the inner being by passing through the Earth's 'vibration'.

Whereas the small Black Virgin statuette inside the church at Myans faces south-west, the huge visible Virgin stands on the tower and, according to the staff in the shop alongside the church, protects the valley below. In fact, by doing so, she is facing north-east [see plate 6]. So the Seal of Solomon does have a practical as well as symbolic value in this area. I was later able to reproduce this significant geometric figure in the landscape of the Chartreuse and further important symbolism of this six-pointed star will be stated at that point.

The Black Virgins are supposed to capture the energy from the Earth through their 'enlarged' hands. This idea has been passed down to healers who transmit magnetic energy through the laying-on of hands. So the bigger the hands, the greater her power. Miracles are supposed to happen around Black Virgins and legends abound throughout the land about their alleged powers. So when the collapsed debris from Mt Granier stopped at the portals of the church, the Black Virgin did not have to enhance her reputation by many other means. The lie of the land could also have had something to do with the church's miraculous escape! However, this church at Myans is the main pilgrimage site in the Chambéry area.

**Plate 6: Notre Dame de Myans, partially obscured
by trees. This view is looking south towards Mt Granier in
the background. Notice the statue of the Virgin, orientated
towards the north-west and thereby symbolically protecting
the Chambéry valley.**

## A new hypothesis on Mt Granier

The two remaining major peaks of the surrounding area
with as yet almost no mention of direct alignments are the
Pointe de la Galoppaz and Mt Granier itself – or rather the
peak of the cliff extension – which collapsed into the valley
in 1248. The actual summit of Mt Granier is hidden behind
the skyline and is unremarkable.

Just as you approach Myans from the west, the Pointe de
la Galoppaz slips behind the wooded elongated summital
ridge of Mt Montgelas whose own actual summit is unpre-
possessing and barely distinguishable. Yet the Pointe de la
Galoppaz has an unusual conical aspect and is very striking
from the south. It towers alongside the neighbouring
mountains in this southern edge of the Bauges and cannot
rightly be ignored.

The pre-1248 outline of Mt Granier is unknown, as no
sketches or lithographs of it before then exist. However, in
his recent book, *L'Effondrement du Mt Granier en Savoie*

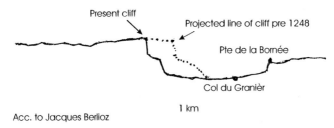

Acc. to Jacques Berlioz

**Figure 5: The presumed outline of Mt. Granier's north-west cliff-face before 1248, (taken from the book by Jacques Berlioz).**

*(1248)*, Jacques Berlioz has added a small diagram on page 39 which gives his idea of what the actual cliff looked like pre-1248 [see figure 5]. It extends some way inwards towards the col – no surprise there!

When I drew a line from the summit of the Pointe de la Galoppaz through Myans, I discovered that it met the 'extended' cliff-line of Mt Granier exactly where the tree-line meets the rocky terrain leading up towards the present peak [see figure 6]. This could be just another coincidence, but they keep mounting up. Although the Pointe de la Galoppaz is just out of sight, its 'influence' could still be important to the builders of Myans, and to the south the obvious target would have been the original stark outline of Mt Granier. In fact, this alignment passes within a 100m. or so of the actual summit of Mt Montgelas and goes over the top of the shoulder leading to it – a recognisable position in its own right. So, with the actual outline of Mt Granier very apparent, I now had a very definite indication as to how far the previous cliff extended towards the Col.

### The last big alignment in the Chambéry valley

While perusing the view from the top of Mt St Michel towards Bellecombe, it was apparent that the significant hill on which the Château at les Marches was built was in line with the remains of the Tours de Chignin – a huge ancient encampment whose only vestiges now are some

21

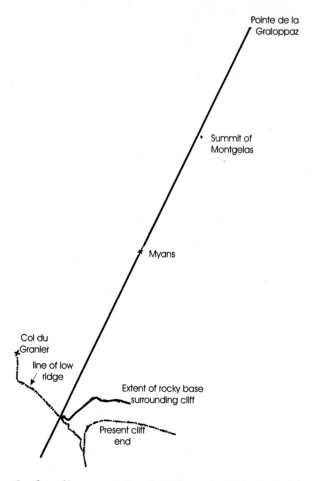

**Figure 6: the alignment starting from la Pointe de la Galoppaz and reaching Mt. Granier [pre-1248], passing through Myans.**

ruined towers amid private vineyards, apart from the afore-mentioned church dedicated to St Anthelme. This line lies almost directly south and to the left of the Bellecombe one as seen from the Mt St Michel chapel. Taking a line from the centre of the Château on the hill at les Marches, it went through the Tours de Chignin and the angle it made with the Bellecombe alignment was 15° [see figure 7]. This was to be of great importance later on.

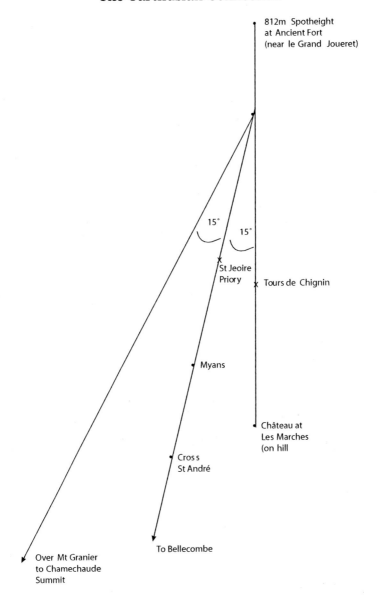

**Figure 7: The alignments between Mt St Michel, the Château des Marches, and Bellecombe. The adjoining 15° angle to the west provides the alignment which leads to the summit of Chamechaude, at some distance in the Chartreuse.**

Interestingly, the extension of this line to the north of Mt St Michel cut through the 812m. trig. point on top of the ancient hill-fort near the Grand Joueret just outside Curienne. Four physical features in line were another apparent vindication of my investigation.

# PART TWO: INTO THE CHARTREUSE

## *Quandary*

I had started out to see if I could find any possible reasons why Myans was situated where it is – apart from the traditional ones given – using a system of alignments and geometric criteria to link up physical features. I now considered that I had done so, but some other interesting facts had surfaced about the past of the Chambéry valley that linked it historically to St Hugues of Grenoble and thence to the Carthusian religious centre of the Chartreuse monastery: Hugues' re-establishing of Myans and St Jeoire; the Black Virgins at Myans and la Grande Chartreuse; the use of the Seal of Solomon which seemed to fit very well with the passage of the sun over the valley; then the alignments joining the Bauges and the Chartreuse, two well-defined separate massifs. I felt that I could go no further immediately in the 'Cluse de Chambéry', but the suspicion remained that the *physical* alignments that led into the Chartreuse really echoed the *historical* clues between the two. So I began to look more closely at the Chartreuse massif, trying to detect any discernible geometric pattern in the landscape and using the religious history as an aid to this end.

## *First thoughts*

My original 'gun-sight' alignments from the Bauges set me on the right path. The Dent de l'Ours and the Grand Som shelter the Carthusian monastery behind it to the southwest and my alignment led straight to it from Mt St Michel.

25

From the cliff-face fissure in Mt Peney, Chamechaude became the focal point. This is the highest point in the Chartreuse and with its relatively isolated position and pyramidal shape it provides an awesome backdrop to St Pierre de Chartreuse opposite. It stands out so much from the north that it had to be the cornerstone of any geometry linked to the area. So this became the centre of my investigation in this area.

My initial poring over the maps produced a myriad of possibilities that spread over an ever-wider area, even back as far as the Bauges and the northern Vercors, but I reckoned at this stage that the area concerned would have to be much smaller, as any geometric pattern would have been far too large to have any importance for those that could have set it up. Henry Lincoln had marvelled at the apparent expertise of the surveyors in his investigations around Rennes-le-Château, and I realised that the savagery of the landscape in the Chartreuse would have given some horrendous problems to those striving to construct the system in strategic areas. So I turned to the historical accounts of St Hugues of Grenoble helping St Bruno set up his Order to see if there could be any hints.

### First clues

In all the references I could find about the founding of the Order, when St Hugues accompanied the monks up into the most deserted spot of the Chartreuse to set up their first huts, the terminology used to describe this almost para-normal event stressed two ideas: firstly, that the area and the actual site were an almost pre-ordained natural temple; secondly, that the dream of St Hugues involving seven stars guided him to the place along with the parallel idea of the sky providing answers to his queries [see figure 12].

My anticipation increased with these two facets of a 'temple' and the sky/stars providing a guide. It is stated that the seven stars seen by St Hugues in his dream were at once connected to the fact that St Bruno arrived with six

Origo Ordinis Cartusiensis
Justo dei indicio accusatus sum
Justo d.i. indicatus sum
Justo d.i. condemnatus sum

Figure 12: **Extracts from the Statuta, printed by Amorbach in 1510, representing episodes in the life of St Bruno. The detail in the seventh extract is enlightening. St Hugues is depicted leading St Bruno and his companions up into the Chartreuse, guided by the seven stars. [Bibliothèque de Grenoble]**

companions, but could there be more to it than this simple correlation? The Hermetic idea of 'as above, so below' was coming back into focus, with star and geometric patterns being of paramount importance.

### The accounts of the founding

I have given my own translations of the following French sources:

From Alexandre Vialate *Légendes (des Montagnes) Vertigineuses du Dauphiné*:

> 'But St Hugues who was the bishop of Grenoble after having been Bruno's pupil, looked up ... to consult the sky, and the sky gave him its answer as it always does when looked at with faith and its reply was a strange dream: St Hugues saw himself transported into the shadows of the night in the midst of the Chartreuse mountains. There, in a clearing surrounded by pine trees and overlooked by threatening rocks, in the middle of boulders broken in the roar of avalanches, it appeared to him that the Lord was building a magnificent temple for Himself. At the same time he saw seven brightly-shining stars stop over the top of the pious building and bathe it in light. The next day Bruno, with six companions, prostrated himself at St Hugues' feet, telling him that attracted from afar by his renowned wisdom, they had come to look for a deserted place to shelter from the storms of this world ...'

From J-C. Krikorian *La Tradition Vivante – St Bruno et Les Chartreux*:

> 'At this time, he (St Hugues) had had a dream: God was building for Himself, in the Chartreuse massif – then a deserted place – an edifice for his glory, and seven stars were showing him the way.'

From Gabriel le Bras *Les Ordres Religieux la vie et l'art*:

> '... A prophetic dream in which he had seen seven stars set in a circle cutting a path for him in the forsaken

*backwoods of his diocese where God Himself was building a temple.'*

From *La Grande Chartreuse par un Chartreux*:

*'Very recently Hugues had seen in a dream God constructing a building in the "desert" of the Chartreuse and seven stars showing him the way. The Bishop in person guided our travellers, following the path which had been revealed to him in the dream, and led them to the site chosen by God.'*

From *La Grande Chartreuse par un Chartreux:*

*'He saw seven stars fall at his feet, then rise up, cross deserted mountains to stop finally in a savage spot called Chartreuse. Hugues then noticed that angels, on God's Command, were constructing a building in this isolated place, and on its roof there appeared again the seven mysterious stars.'*

From E. Margaret Thompson *The Carthusian Order in England*:

*'Hugues received them graciously, and with reverence, for he had had a dream not long before of a dwelling-place of God's Honour being built in a certain spot whither seven stars had led him among the mountains . . . without hesitation, on observing that there were seven strangers, and connecting them with the seven stars, he guided them to the place of his dream, the solitude of La Chartreuse.'*

So, St Hugues had set out from Grenoble, taken the route leading up through Corenc, crossed the Col de Portes, and the green Chartreuse pastures, and arrived at the entrance to the 'désert', according to M.A.Pascal *Le désert de la Grande Chartreuse.*

The route was known and the area was quite closely limited to that surrounding St Pierre de Chartreuse. I felt that there had to be some geometric pattern based on this relatively small area , and of which Chamechaude would be the cornerstone, with the Grand Som inextricably linked with it.

### *A connection with Mt St Michel*

Thinking of the connection between the Bauges and the Chartreuse and hoping for inspiration, I looked back at my last two alignments in the Chambéry valley: those from Mt St Michel to the south leading to les Marches and to Bellecombe. Another line drawn at 15° to the south-west would lead directly to the Chartreuse over Mt Granier, [figure 7].

I continued this line which passed over the north-eastern spur of Mt Granier to reach within 50 m or so of the summit of Mt Pinet, over the cliff-face of Colleret and on down towards Chamechaude. The closer I approached the latter, the more amazed I became, as this line hit the summit of Chamechaude exactly. I realise that putting 1:25000 maps together is a difficult operation when trying to be precise but my checks were verified. This alignment was precise but had little to add in its projection south-west.

I decided to take a 15° angle back to the north-east from Chamechaude as a parallel manoeuvre to the initial steps in the Chambéry valley. This line then struck the Lances de Malissard directly between the two peaks – the Lance Nord and the Lance Sud. It was then that I felt that I had discovered a base-line to start linking up the area.

What was now standing out from the map was the realisation that the mountains around St Pierre de Chartreuse encircled it: Chamechaude and the Grand Som in the south and north; the Lances de Malissard to the north-east; the Dent de Crolles to the south-east; the Charmant Som to the west/south-west; and the Rocher du Solitaire/the Roches des Molières to the north-west. This then had to be important to the geometry. Whether five or six peaks could be considered more or less important, surely this configuration could qualify as a basis for a 'holy' area or a figurative

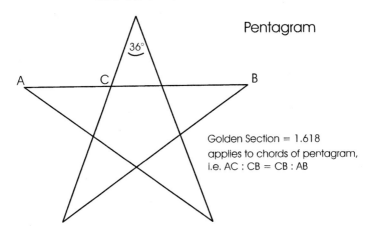

**Figure 8: The pentagram (five-pointed star): each angle is 36°. The Golden Section is an integral part of the geometry.**

'temple'. It was as if the area was protected by these mountains surrounding it.

The idea of five mountains immediately led me to the notion of a pentagram [see figure 8], so using my base-line from Chamechaude to the Lances de Malissard, I constructed it as best I could, using ordinary instruments.

### First placing of the pentagram

It would be too much to hope that the five peaks would fall magically into place to fit the five-pointed star, but the result was not too far removed from respectability.

The north point struck a position a couple of hundred metres to the west of the summit of the Grand Som, but high up on the upper slopes nonetheless. The western arm went across the north flank of the Charmant Som to end up in a nondescript point in the upper forest, while the south-east point ended up in the Neyroud on the south-east flank of the Dent de Crolles. But the diagonal from the Grand Som did run down the summital cliff-face ridge of the Dent de Crolles and pass very close to the actual highest point. However, the diagonals crossed in inauspicious places and the actual middle point of the whole pentagram was lost in the forest to the immediate east of St Hugues de Chartreuse.

The only other point of interest was the upper east-west diagonal whose mid-point was very close indeed to the present church in St Pierre de Chartreuse. Was this coincidence?

I decided that there were not enough exact coincidences to come to any real conclusion, but the feeling was very firmly established that I was on the right lines. I would find this to be true later.

### *Meaning of the pentagram*

The reason why I was examining the possibility of this particular geometric pattern was first and foremost a result of my interest in Henry Lincoln's investigations around Rennes-le-Château. The pentagram has been associated with occult and religious ceremony throughout the ages. To quote Henry Lincoln himself in his book *Key to the Sacred Pattern*:

> *The pentagon and the pentagram . . . have enjoyed immense prestige and excited nothing short of reverence among geometers, architects, and masons since very ancient times. For the Pythagoreans (c. sixth century BC), the pentagram was a symbol of life, eternity and health . . . The use of the pentagram in later magical practice, as a protection against uninvited spiritual agencies is, presumably, a reminiscence of, or direct inheritance from, the Pythagorean tradition.*
>
> *The stars and planets were, of course, of enormous interest and importance to medieval scholars. Indeed, such enquiries began in remote antiquity. Babylon, as well as Egypt and ancient China have left us evidence of highly skilled and detailed astronomical studies. The great stone monuments of Carnac in France and Stonehenge in Britain also show that complex astronomical work had been undertaken in megalithic*

*times. Yet again, we must not allow our modern knowledge of the workings of the cosmos to affect our reaction to our ancestors' understanding. For them, the heavens were the home of the gods and became, in Christian times, the holy place where dwelt God and all his saints.*

*As they turned, the planets were showing us the mysterious workings of God's hand, expressed in the harmonious movement of the spheres. One aspect of that ancient study related to the invisible patterns which the planets draw across the firmament . . . Only one planet shows us a perfect geometric form. The form is pentagonal and the planet is Venus. Creating five equally spaced alignments over a period of eight years, she draws the perfect, hidden and secret symbol of the five-pointed star in the heavens . . . knowledge which would have been accessible 'only to the initiated'. . . Here is a sacred place.*

On referring to the *Encyclopédie d'Aujourd'hui,* I found the following comments about the pentagram in the section *Encyclopédie des Symboles*:

- for Pythagoreans, it was a sacred sign symbolising the harmony of the body and soul (and therefore a sign of health);
- for Manichean Gnostics, whose sacred number was five, it was a sacred symbol: the five elements represented were: light – air – wind – fire – water;
- in Christian iconography, the five points represent the five wounds of Christ. Its closed form (equalling a circle) represents the start and end of all things in Christ;
- where it was painted/scored in house thresholds, it was supposed to ward off demons or evil spirits.

Then Greg Rigby, to whose book, *On Earth as it is in Heaven,* I shall return later, describes it thus:

*'The figure has been associated with occultists, the Ancient Mysteries and more recently with Jesus Christ. Pythagoreans were aware of its link to the Golden Section (Q = 1.618) which has been described as a "geometers'*

*hymn". This proportion, often referred to in the context of sacred geometry, was much used in the construction of the Gothic cathedrals'*

He then quoted John Mitchell, *The Dimensions of Paradise*:

*'Christian mystics made the pentagram an emblem of Jesus, who fed 5000 with five loaves and two fishes and who represents the archetypal man (with five senses and five fingers on each hand). Its esoteric connection with the crucified man is given further point by the fact that the square on the height of the five-pointed star, contained in a pentagon with each side measuring one unit, is equal to 2.368 square units, 2368 being the number of Jesus Christ.'*

Manly P.Hall *The Secret Teachings of all Ages*, is quoted also by Rigby:

*'The pentagram is the formula of the microcosm – the magical formula of man. It is the one, rising out of the four – the human soul rising out of the bondage of animal nature. It is the true light – the "Star of the Morning". It marks the centre of five mysterious centres of force, the awakening of which is the supreme secret of white magic.'*

The number 5 (the number of the sides and angles of the pentagram) had a special significance in ancient times. In *The Serpent in the Sky* by J.A.West:

*'To the Pythagoreans, **five** was the number of "love" or "life", because it represented the union of the first male number, **three**, with the first female number, **two**. Four terms are necessary to account for the idea of matter, or substance. But these four terms are insufficient to account for its creation. It is **five**, the union of male and female, that enables it to "happen". Hence the pentagram and pentagon have been revered as sacred symbols throughout the ages. In ancient Egypt, the symbol for a star was drawn with five points. The ideal of the realised man was to become a star, and to become "one of the company of Ra".*

*The pentagram, made up of the Golden Section*

*segments, is the symbol of unremitting activity; "five" is the key to the vitality of the Universe, its creative nature. In mundane terms, "four" accounts for the fact of the sculptor's statue, but does not account for the "doing" of it. Five terms are required to account for the principle of "creation"; "5" is accordingly the number of "potentiality". Potentiality exists outside time. "5" is therefore the number of eternity and the principle of eternal creation, union of male and female – and it is for this reason, and along these lines of thought, that the Ancients came to hold "5" in what looks to us like a peculiar reverence.'*

Because of all these wide-ranging explanations, which have been present throughout various epochs and differing cultures, including Christianity, I felt that the pentagram was a real possibility for a starting-point.

### Why this location for St Bruno?

If all this was known to St Bruno, then a site which had all the potential of spirituality because of its physical and geographical layout would have appeared to be an optimum one in which to found a small gathering of like-minded hermits. Their own spirituality would have been echoed by the 'holiness' of their surroundings and this might have given them some impetus to take the initial steps. But their first huts were constructed just to the north-west of the initial pentagram and outside the pentagon. This would surely have been due to the fact that they wanted to cut themselves off as far as possible from external influences, so they sought a site as inaccessible as possible, but within 'range' of the spiritual shadow of the pentagonal layout of the mountains. The village of St Pierre de Chartreuse was within this latter area. In fact, St Bruno and his companions had help from the inhabitants of St Pierre and la Ruchère while they were getting themselves established. Their initial site was truly inhospitable.

Jean Billet in *Le Guide de la Chartreuse*, states that St Pierre de Chartreuse was first a hamlet near the bridge and therefore a crossing point at La Diat. He says that the choice of site was determined by the presence of water and the desire to avoid too much contact with the existing village communities.

The Archivist of la Grande Chartreuse, D. Luc. Fauchon, says that the most important considerations were the presence of water, of wood for construction and heating, and of austere surroundings.

Peter Dawkins, a consultant and specialist in Zoence (Science of Life and Earth Harmony), made the telling remark that the Carthusians held a great knowledge concerning *land* and *water energies*, and used that knowledge, so it would be surprising if their sites were not carefully located. There would seem to be scope for all conditions to be met.

### Plan 'B' – the Seal of Solomon

However I moved the pentagram around, I could not make any really convincing coincidental points obvious. So some lateral thinking was necessary. Suppose the geometry depended initially on something very similar to the pentagram? Then the memory of the Seal of Solomon returned from Myans. Even though I had made the connection with Myans at its re-emergence with St Hugues after the founding of St Bruno's site, the principle would have been present long before.

So I applied the same base-line between Chamechaude and the Lances de Malissard. The remaining north-west point of the south-facing triangle lay just beyond the Roche du Solitaire, but the line cut through the ridge very close to the peak itself.

The north point of the other upper triangle was in a small high valley just north-east of the Grand Som and south-east of the Dent de l'Ours. The south-west line passed within a hundred or so metres to the north of the Grand Som itself and came to its point at the Col de la Charmette – precisely! I wondered if could be coincidence that there is an oratoire at this exact spot, i.e. a marker stone/shrine, showing the limits of the territory belonging to the monks.

The south-east triangular point was closer to the Dent de Crolles, but also followed the cliff-top very close to the actual summit, while the south base-line passed through the Col du Coq. This time I felt much closer to a 'good fit', with three precise points out of six, while the inter-connecting lines for the two triangles highlighted other main physical features. Further investigation with this basic parameter was now needed.

On joining the north-west and north triangle points, I noticed that this line crossed through the *exact site* of Notre Dame de Casalibus, where St Bruno had established his

**Plate 7: The whole central valley of the Chartreuse, from the summit of Chamechaude, looking north towards the Bauges in the distance. The most distant clearly visible peak to the right is Mt Margeriaz; the further of the two U-shaped cols is the col du Granier, with the Granier on its right; the nearer col is Col du Coucheron; the Grand Som is the mountain on the left. Note the gun-sight effect down to the right of the Grand Som's peak, at the upper limit of the forest; the small U-shaped col is the Col des Aures, through which the main bisecting line of the hexagram and pentagram passes directly to the Roche Veyrand, seen here clipping the top of the trees at the right-hand apex of the col des Aures.**

**Plate 8: A Carthusian oratory, at the Col de la Charmette. This is the point which corresponds to the south-west point of the Seal of Soloman.**

**Plate 9: The Dent de Crolles, from the south-east, alongside the motorway, north-east of Grenoble. Its gigantic silhouette draws the eye from a great distance.**

first settlement. Again, could this be pure coincidence? Was there any further reasoning behind the fact that the northern triangle's point was again not planted directly on the summit of the Grand Som? [see plate 7] This line of thought was to be very important.

### The importance of the Seal of Solomon

After much time spent trying to discover the symbolic meaning of the Seal of Solomon without finding much of direct relevance, two sources gave me some encouragement. A dictionary of symbols in France made the link between the Seal of Solomon and his 'Hymn of Hymns': the latter's traditional Christian interpretation is that it represents, firstly, the love uniting Christ and the Church; and, secondly, the mystical union of the soul with the basic divine principle. This would have been of paramount importance to St Bruno who had renounced all material trappings to be able to commune with God in extreme solitude, but who was still highly regarded by the Pope. To have this physical link with the author of such an important tract around him in his self-imposed solitude would surely have been a source of solace to him.

The second source I found in Robert Bauval's *Secret Chamber*. In it he refers to *The Hiram Key* by Christopher Knight and Robert Lomas, – and their interpretation of the 'Star of David' i.e. the Seal of Solomon:

*'The star of David is today fully accepted as the symbol of Judaism but the hexagram is actually two symbols superimposed to create a new, composite meaning, and its origin is not Jewish at all. The top and bottom points of this star are the apex of two pyramids, overlaid one upon the other. The upward pointing pyramid is an ancient symbol for the power of a king, with its base resting on Earth and its summit reaching to Heaven. The other represents the power of the priest, established in Heaven and reaching down to Earth . . . As such it is the only true sign of Jesus, and it carries the extra meaning as being representative of the bright star of David's line that arose*

*in the morning. It is called the star of David, not because David invented it, but because Jesus used it and he positioned himself to be the "Star of David" that had been prophesied. . .'*

Bauval comments further to say:

*'In actual fact, the predominant esoteric layer of meaning in the "Star of David" symbol is that it symbolises the completion or fulfilment of the "Work" which humanity must undertake in order to reunite with God. As such, Jesus the Messiah in the Christian mysteries is the epicentral figure who is deemed to have initiated the decisive turning point in the "Work" for humanity to accomplish in His name.'*

As St Bruno was one of the most enlightened sages of his time, the above symbolism would have been known to him. What better place could be found to continue Jesus' work than here, where the solitude would answer his own yearning and the inherent symbolic geometric layout of the surrounding mountains would provide the perfect setting for the 'Work' to be undertaken?

### Another Cardinal Point

When I looked beyond the northern triangular point of this Seal of Solomon, I realised that it was 'pointing' directly towards the most distinctive peak overlooking and dominating the town of St Pierre d'Entremont – the Roche Veyrand [see plate 7]. The cliff-face rears up over the valley of the Guiers Vif and is a beacon in its own right.

Indeed, the line bisecting this northern triangular point from Chamechaude arrived perfectly on cue at the summit. Again, this could not be pure coincidence. The clinching fact then was an eye-opener: on measuring the line from Chamechaude to the Roche Veyrand, the distance between the southern and northern points of the Seal of Solomon was almost exactly twice that from the northern point to the Roche Veyrand. Or the distance was almost exactly divisible into three sections: from Chamechaude to the centre of the hexagram; from here to the northern point; from the latter to the summit of the Roche Veyrand. This was the reason why the northern triangular point of the hexagram did not meet up directly with the summit of the Grand Som. This equi-distancing, within the confines of working across large distances on two juxtaposed maps, and the alignment convinced me that I was on the right track.

Four other points along this line then became apparent: the line crosses the bridge/road at its junction with the river at La Diat – the initial settlement of St Pierre de Chartreuse; it crosses the Col des Aures, just to the east of the Grand Som; it passes through the chapel of Notre Dame de la Paix and fringes the Château du Gouvernement just above and to the south of St Pierre d'Entremont. So this alignment was certainly highlighted.

### From Chamechaude towards Grenoble

Perhaps this bisecting line could produce something unexpected in the other direction. Accordingly, I continued to the south of Chamechaude. Sure enough, the line passed through the church at Sappey-en-Chartreuse [see plate 14], cut through the cliff ridge of St Eynard close to the present position of the Fort, passed within 50m or so of a church in Corenc and hit the Isère river in the same distance as the diameter of the Seal of Solomon, [see figure 9]. I felt that the correspondence of the church at Sappey was too precise to be coincidental. Some expert surveying techniques were being displayed here.

### From the Roche Veyrand

Looking at this bisecting line more closely, I noticed that it passed through the Col des Aures near the northern triangular point. From Chamechaude at 2082m, then through the Col at approximately 1650m, to reach the summit of the Roche Veyrand at 1429m, I reasoned that the same 'gun-sight' effect might be apparent from the latter. Sure enough, after slogging up the unforgiving path one hot morning (with a distinctly uncomprehending son in tow)

**Plate 14: The church at Sappey-en-Chartreuse, with Chamechaude's northern cliffs behind. This is marked by the third star of the Plough's handle, Alioth.**

there was the pointed peak of Chamechaude highlighted towards the left edge in the U-shaped upper valley to the left of the Grand Som. The repetition of this motif was proof enough to my eyes that the fortuitous lay-out of the geography lent itself to some amazing surveying possibilities. So the summit of the Grand Som did not have to be exactly targeted for the alignment to be of paramount importance.

What else could be of importance to the siting of St Bruno's settlement with regard to the Roche Veyrand and the sacred geometric ideal?

Taking the line from this peak through the present position of the Chapelle St Bruno, it soon reached another point which was to be of great importance to the Order as an 'entrance-gate' to their territory – this is an amazing huge separate needle-like pillar of rock jammed against the road

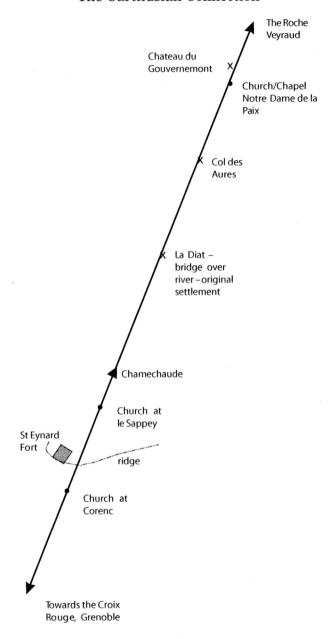

The Roche
Veyraud

Chateau du
Gouvernemont

Church/Chapel
Notre Dame de la
Paix

Col des
Aures

La Diat –
bridge over
river – original
settlement

Chamechaude

Church at
le Sappey

St Eynard
Fort

ridge

Church at
Corenc

Towards the Croix
Rouge, Grenoble

**Figure 9: The alignment between the Roche Veyrand and Grenoble, passing through the Col des Aures, Chamechaude and the church at le Sappey.**

**Plate 10: The Pic de l'Oeillette, formerly an important entrance gate for the Carthusians.**

leading up from St Laurent du Pont. This is the Pic de l' Oeillette [see plate 10], where travellers and visitors had to be checked for weapons before being allowed through into Chartreux monks' land. The accuracy of the line was very thought-provoking, especially as the Pic de l'Oeillette is hidden behind a huge promontary to the north.

### *The pentagram returns*

When I measured the angle between the bisecting line from Chamechaude to the Roche Veyrand and this new one to the Pic de l'Oeillette, I was again surprised to find it equalling 18°, half that of each angle of a pentagram (36°). So I began constructing the pentagram whose northern point was

44

the Roche Veyrand and which overlapped the Seal of Solomon.

The north-western point falls near the road from St Laurent du Pont to the Marine, behind some newer houses at the Moulins. It was hard to investigate much here, but there was what seemed to be an old track leading to the scattered base stones of an old building. This was as close as I could get, but as yet I have no further information as to what this ruined square outline and mound represent. Could some marker have existed hereabouts beforehand?

The south-eastern point again fell in the wooded slopes immediately north of Perquelin where the road now ends. What it does highlight is the start of the 'Cirque' which is explored by the GR9, but I was again frustrated in a minute search for some tangible evidence on the ground by private property and fences.

The last point – to the north-east – was again an exciting find. At the exact distance required from the Pic de l'Oeillette, there is a cross marked on the map along the GR9. Working out the exact angle across juxtaposed maps nowadays is never easy, but this one for any ancient surveying must have been a nightmare as there is no possibility of any line of sight as huge wooded ridges and mountains intervene. It was close enough by my reckoning, i.e. to within 1°. Added to this precise positioning was the question as to why the cross is here anyway.

I went to find it. It is 100m from the junction of two paths – the GR9 and the one which winds up from the Pas de la Mort in the Cirque St Même. There is no obvious reason for a cross here, even though what I had expected to turn out to be an erected wooden cross is in fact *a stone with the Carthusian emblem* [see plate 11]. Its good condition is no doubt attributable to the Office National des Forêts who periodically bring all the paths and signs up to scratch. On enquiring at the Syndicats d'Initiatives at both St Pierre d'Entremont and St Pierre de Chartreuse they both confirmed that it was indeed the Carthusian cross, but that it was too far away from the monastery to delineate its territory. The same answer came from the bookshop at the

**Plate 11: The cross itself, beside the GR9 path, engraved in a rock. It shows the Carthusian emblem, but why here, when it is named after St Hugon, far away to the north-east?**

Correrie (the official monastery museum), where a blank was drawn for any other reason.

Further research from *Les Chartreux – le désert et le monde: 1084–1984*, showed that the original territory accorded to the Chartreux was limited to the Cluse (valley) in which St Bruno established his first settlement. To the east it was limited to the summital ridge of the Grand Som. A 1649 map from the Archives Départementales de l'Isère shows that it had not changed. I could not get any further definite information as to whether the territory had been increased since then, but such a huge extra distance seems very unlikely.

Could my geometric answer be the actual original reason for it being there? Again, three exact points from five seemed a very reasonable score for my pentagram, especially as the initial line drawn crossed through the first site established by St Bruno. In addition, on joining the two southern points, the line passed through the other 'gateway' to St Pierre de

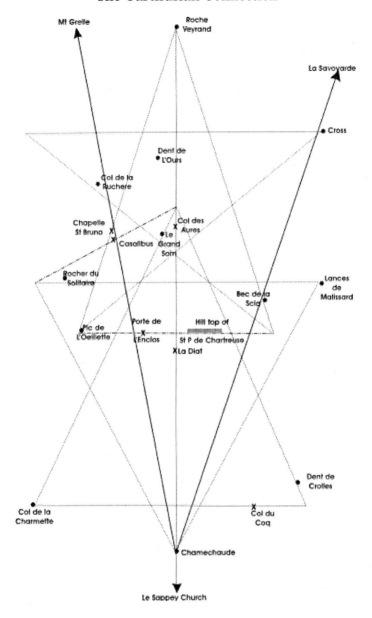

**Figure 10: The pentagram and the Seal of Solomon superimposed. Note the intersection of the three lines passing through la Chapelle St Bruno and Notre-Dame de Casalibus.**

47

Chartreuse – the Porte de l'Enclos, a narrow defile in the ridge between the Grand Som and the Charmant Som. It also cut through the centre of St Pierre de Chartreuse.

If I was right, then the whole area was seen to be a vast natural 'temple' using both the Seal of Solomon and the pentagram to confirm its validity [see figure 10]. The combined importance of both could only have enhanced its attraction for a religious order to be started here.

## A confirmatory overview

The link between the Chartreuse and the Cluse de Chambéry was again confirmed by a huge triangle between three main points already mentioned

A line just east of north from Chamechaude, drawn through both chapels of the original settlement (St Bruno and Casalibus) passes directly through the Col de la Ruchère and ultimately reaches the summit of Mt Grelle [see figure 10].

Another line from Chamechaude drawn through this 'outcast' cross on the GR9 meets the Roche du Guet at the point (i.e. just above the Savoyarde) where the east-west line arrives from Mt Grelle, cutting through Myans [see figure 3 page 9]. Could this be another reason for the positioning of this 'odd' cross? In addition, as the original site of St Bruno's settlement was now seen to be lying on the intersection of three lines, I duly considered the evidence was mounting.

On visiting the above chapels, I was further intrigued to find a pentagram incorporated into the design on the underside of each porch. How far could coincidence go? Once again, no-one at the Correrie could answer my query as to why they should be there, even though the chapels have been renovated on occasions over the last few centuries.

In his letter to me, the Archivist of la Grande Chartreuse, D. Luc Fauchon, was somewhat embarrassed at having no idea, apart from them being possibly simple ornamental design motifs. Again, an illuminating, but unanswered discovery!

48

# PART THREE: THE HISTORICAL SEARCH FOR ST BRUNO'S ARRIVAL

## A step backwards

I was convinced that this part of the Chartreuse was a 'temple' with the alignments, the pentagram and the hexagram (Seal of Solomon) all interconnected to produce a natural source of spirituality that could be 'harnessed' by a mind-set far removed from our own; a new life could be begun by St Bruno, whose saintliness would echo and merge with the physical potential of the site for this very purpose. But was his arrival here a pure coincidence, or was it a planned journey from Reims where he was on the verge of being made the new Archbishop?

Looking back at St Bruno's exit from Reims and his subsequent travels to the Chartreuse would have to be the next stage to see if there were any hints as to why he came here before all other possible destinations.

## St Bruno: from Reims onwards

Manassès had been the corrupt and vengeful former Archbishop of Reims with whom St Bruno had locked horns and generally been on the receiving end of his scheming. However, Bruno refused to give in and the corrupt Manassès was eventually exposed and disgraced, and then exiled. Hence Bruno was received back with jubilation into the hearts of the clergy and the people who acclaimed him as their next Archbishop. This would be the summit of his achievement in probably the most important bishopric in France, where he had already made his mark with ranks of increasing importance. And yet he turned his back on it, to become a hermit in one of the wildest spots possible!

I have used the distinguished book by André Ravier *St Bruno le Chartreux*, as my basic reference, as he has tried to pierce the host of legends and myths that have grown up over the centuries about this extraordinary figure and he has worked closely in tandem with the monks' research at La Grande Chartreuse itself.

Are there any hints in Bruno's education that would have made him aware of the possibilities offered by the Chartreuse? D. Luc Fauchon, the Archiviste of the Monastery, answered my query by stating that Bruno would have been well aware of astronomy. He was one of the 'Litterati', who would therefore have followed lessons in the studies of the 'Trivium' and the 'Quadrivium'. Astronomy was one of the subjects taught. Ravier goes into further detail. Reims, at the time of Bruno's education, was at the pinnacle of its standards of knowledge and education, as students flocked there from Germany, Italy and all Europe. Knowledge was encyclopaedic and 'Human Science' served as a preamble to theology. The Trivium was grammar, rhetoric and philosophy. The student then passed to the Quadrivium i.e. arithmetic, music, *geometry* and *astronomy*. Then came theology – the crowning of all human knowledge. But what parts of geometry and astronomy were taught at that time? From the Druidic tradition onwards, via Pythagoras, Plato and other Greek mathematicians, and the later Celtic teachings, these principles would not have been unknown to Bruno. Hence the Ancient Mysteries and their traditions would have been available for assimilation. Indeed, mathematics and geometry were regarded by the Pagan sages as sacred sciences that reveal the workings of the Mind of God.

Bruno had a change of heart when faced with his decision at Reims. He realised that he was called to serve God, but not at Reims:

*'We talked about the false attractions and the perishable riches of this world and of the joys of eternal glory. So, burning with divine love, we promised, vowed, decided to*

50

*leave soon the fleeting shadows of the century to search for
eternal blessings and take up monastic clothing.' [Bruno
later writing about a conversation he had with Raoul le
Verd]*

So a momentous decision was taken. Surely, would not a
special place to carry out his vow have been one of his
preoccupations?

### The First Move

Bruno and his two companions left Reims between 1081 and
1083 to go south, towards Troyes. They stopped at the Abbey
of Molesmes, where St Robert was Abbot of the Benedictine
monks. Bruno's party was put up at Sèche-Fontaine, a few
kms away, a previously unused establishment. It was far
enough away for them to feel sufficiently cut off from outside
interference, but close enough for easy relations to be
continued with St Robert. They stayed here between one to
three years, before the growth of Molesmes forced Bruno to
choose between being assimilated by it, or to continue on his
search for a hermit's life. His two companions opted to stay,
but Bruno left. Yet Bruno and Robert always held each other
in high esteem. Robert went on to found Cîteaux in 1098,
before returning to Molesmes in 1099. So he began the
Cistercian Order.

### The Principal Move

Ravier states very clearly that Bruno continued south
towards Grenoble and the Alps *and that the reasons for this
choice are unknown.* It is here that various authors have put
forward different ideas:

E. Margaret Thompson *The Carthusian Order in England:*

*'On the advice of Seguin, Abbot of the Benedictine Abbey
of La Chaise-Dieu, who gave them letters of introduction,
Bruno and six companions went to a former novice of
that abbey, Hugues de Châteauneuf, Bishop of Grenoble.
Hugues had spent a year at La Chaise-Dieu, trying*

*out the monastic life, before being told to return to Grenoble.'*

Bernard Bligny *St Bruno, le premier Chartreux*:

*'The Papal Legate, Hugues, who became Archbishop of Lyon in 1082, had put Hugues de Grenoble in charge there in 1080. Did Hugues de Lyon talk to Bruno about his former fellow "disciple", Seguin, who was made Abbot of La Chaise-Dieu in 1078 and who stayed friends with him? We don't know.'*

Bligny also states that Hugues de Lyon knew Robert de Molesmes, but that Bruno did not know Hugues de Grenoble.

H. Löbbel and Abbé Lefèvre, in *St Bruno et l'Ordre des Chartreux*:

*'Bruno and Seguin knew each other since the time that Seguin was in Reims to carry out reforms in the Abbey of St Nicaise. But the marginal date given for this is 1090, evidently far too late. However, Bruno and Seguin may have met at Reims or elsewhere before Seguin was occupied with the Abbey of St Nicaise . . . The links with Seguin continue. The land on which Bruno was building his settlement (i.e. in the Chartreuse) belonged to certain people, among them Seguin. But he, on Hugues' suggestion, renounced his rights in a charter. When Bruno was called to be a counsellor to his former pupil, Eudes de Châtillon, now Pope Urbain II, in 1090, his companions were dismayed and decided to follow him. So Bruno, not wishing it to pass to secular uses, made over the Chartreuse to Seguin again. After a while in Rome, they returned to the Chartreuse. Seguin ceded to Landuin, their present superior, and to his successors all their former territory in a deed dated 18th October 1090'.*

Auguste Bouchayer *Les Chartreux, Maîtres de Forge*:

*'The influence of La Chaise-Dieu on the upsurge of our region was considerable. No doubt that they had in their*

*possession the "désert" with the secret thought, one day in the future, of setting up their influence there. The realisation was not long in coming.*

*Seguin was in Reims to reform the Abbey of St Nicaise. He met Bruno there . . . one of the greatest men of his time. He had a considerable influence on Bruno's decision to leave the world behind; more than that, he advised him to settle in the Chartreuse and sent him to the young Bishop of Grenoble, Hugues de Châteauneuf, who, having been a disciple and pupil of Bruno, had formerly been a novice at La Chaise-Dieu.*

*These three 'princes' of the Church, the Elite, were united in one and the same desire – to establish a hermit life in the Chartreuse. Seguin gives up all his rights to the area, Hugues chooses the spot, as shown by the strange appearance of the seven stars . . . Bruno will be the Master of the Order . . . Bruno's plan was conceived before his departure from Reims, the Abbot of La Chaise-Dieu and Bishop Hugues make sure the plan is realised.'*

The whole tenor of this passage reminds us of a plot hatched by scheming high-placed churchmen! And there do seem to be possible inconsistencies.

Auguste Côte, in *La Grande Chartreuse par un Chartreux*, restates the links established between Bruno and Seguin in Reims with regard to St Nicaise, plus Seguin's possessions in the Dauphiné. Seguin's advice to leave for Grenoble because of Hugues and his spending a year as novice at La Chaise-Dieu are stated as being superfluous, as Hugues had been a disciple of Bruno in Reims. The following three authors, M. A. Pascal *Le désert de la Grande Chartreuse*, Marc Dubois, *La Grande Chartreuse: l'art religieux au monastère*, Albert du Boys *La Grande Chartreuse*, all state that St Hugues had been a disciple of Bruno at Reims.

From the *archives of la Chaise-Dieu* at le Puy en Velay, the contention is that, while Hugues was a novice at la Chaise-Dieu, the links established between him and Seguin explain the role played by the latter in the setting up of the

Carthusians. Hugues persuaded Seguin to cede the rights to the land to Bruno on 9 December 1084.

Pierre-Roger Gaussin *Le Rayonnement de la Chaise-Dieu,* has only one comment, which is that the St Nicaise reform was in fact in 1090

Even switching to the latest information on the French Internet, with the website entitled, *Histoire de St Bruno et d'"esikia&quot,* previous ideas are repeated:

> *'Tired of the intrigues and a fraught atmosphere, he [Bruno] took the decision to depart. During this time, his friend Hugues had become Bishop of Grenoble. In their correspondence, the word "hesychia" is often repeated: St Bruno was looking for "a place whose qualities would have a peaceful (indeed spiritual) influence on those who lived there." Making use of his powerful position as Bishop, Hugues persuaded first of all the Benedictines of La Chaise-Dieu to give up the possessions that they had in the region, and some local nobility to exchange places in Paradise for a few hundred hectares. The combined result formed the "désert de la Grande Chartreuse".'*

On this very confused part of Bruno's life, Ravier says that:

1. There is no truth in the idea of Hugues being a disciple of Bruno in Reims. When Bruno was a student there, Hugues was not yet born; when Bruno became 'écolâtre', Hugo was just five years old. Hugo might just have been Bruno's pupil towards the end of his professorship. But if so, why didn't Guigues in his *Life of Bruno* say anything about it?
2. Hugues and Bruno, without probably having ever met, knew about each other and held each other in great esteem.
3. Bruno and his companions went off to Grenoble with just the desire to live near the saintly Hugues.
4. There is no truth in the idea of Seguin influencing Bruno in his decision to go to Grenoble.

My conclusion from all these different ideas is that there

still remains an unresolved link between Sèche-Fontaine, Molesmes and Grenoble. Bruno knew St Robert very well, Hugues had stayed with Seguin at la Chaise-Dieu. Bruno knew of Seguin and had possibly met up with him. Bruno and Hugues had heard of each other and possibly had met. There was Hugues de Lyon as a link in the background. But would these acquaintances have been enough reason in themselves for Bruno to trek all the way to Grenoble in the hope of finding the ideal place to establish a new small settlement? Ravier thinks not. One small hint comes from D. Luc Fauchon in his letter to me from the Chartreuse Archives: that all four men were Litterati and therefore were educated in astronomy and geometry – including ancient traditions.

# PART FOUR: THE CRUCIAL LINK

## *A revelation*

On browsing through the 'France' bookshop at Stow-on-the-Wold, I chanced upon what proved to be a revelatory new publication by Greg Rigby *On Earth as it is in Heaven*. This brought a parallel line of enquiry into focus and proved to be a vital link.

Like him, I had read Louis Charpentier's book on Chartres Cathedral and its mysteries, but his assertion that the Benedictine abbeys of the Caux country trace on Earth the pattern of the 'Great Bear' (Ursus Major) or the 'Plough' did not ring a bell. Rigby goes on to find the 'Great Bear' represented across a huge expanse of the north of France, taking in the cathedrals of Chartres, Bonne Mare, St Quentin, Reims and Verdun, plus sites at Landonvillers and Donnersberg.

He then astutely finds that *within the body of the Plough a perfect pentagram can be formed if the 'arms' are extended to form the pentagon* [see figure 11]. Suddenly the two ideas together hit me like a bolt from the blue.

I had found the pentagram in the Chartreuse. St Hugues' 'dream' of seven stars leading him there now took on a very concrete meaning, apart from the accepted one of St Bruno arriving with six companions.

Referring back to Ravier's very detailed account of this dream, he states that *'it defies the most demanding critical analysis'*.

Guigues, in his *Vie de St Hugues*, written in the most mundane fashion, mentions it because *he was not able, himself, not to believe it.*

56

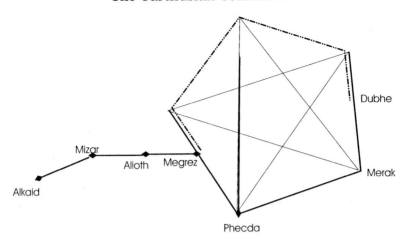

**Figure 11: The pentagram contained within the extended arms of the Plough.**

Ravier describes it in terms of '*an exceptional mystical phenomenon*'. A telling phrase goes on to say that:

> '*The events that followed, the whole history of the Carthusian Order, moreover bear witness to the importance of the role played by the geography of the Chartreuse on the style itself of Carthusian life. Between this mountainous area and this life, there were established deep and determining correspondences.*'

I would add that the founding of the Order was included in this. So, St Hugues' dream was a kind of hidden code, a stellar map to pinpoint the way to this particular and extraordinary spot. *What formation of seven stars could be more obvious in the sky, and more important throughout the ages, particularly with regard to navigation, than the Great Bear?*

I was amazed that these two linked formations should so unexpectedly point me towards further map study, but then, in the same text, another familiar name of singular importance was picked out – *St Robert de Molesmes*.

Rigby investigates most thoroughly the provenance of this representation of the Plough in northern France, firstly when it was designed and constructed. His conclusion is that the Celts or Druids were the 'planners, architects and builders of the earthly Plough' and that its secret existence shows that its construction had great significance amongst the highest orders of Druid priests. Then these sacred sites were taken over by the first Christian Churches and enhanced over the centuries as Catholicism became the dominant form of Christianity. But the initial Druidic layout was not forgotten.

St Robert de Molesmes is singled out by Rigby as the person who most probably brought this knowledge – of the seven sites, the pentagram and the pentagon – back into use in the founding of the first Cistercian Abbeys of Cîteaux and Clairvaux. There are very accurate alignments found by Rigby all over France between abbeys, churches and cathedrals, and the most important early ones are intricately concerned with these two; especially when Cîteaux and Clairvaux were moved by small distances to comply more accurately: Cîteaux, founded in 1098, then moved in 1101; and Clairvaux, founded in 1115, moved in 1135.

Rigby states that such accurate alignments through the abbeys to the pentagram indicate that someone involved in the establishment of Cîteaux and the displacement of Clairvaux Abbey was aware of the Plough and the pentagram it contained. That person, Rigby concludes, after very detailed investigation, could only have been St Robert.

The added fact that the celebrated leader of the Cistercian revival – St Bernard – entered Cîteaux in 1112 and was appointed the Abbot of Clairvaux in 1115 to transform a failing Order into a phenomenally successful one (321 abbeys built in 34 years) in partnership with the Knights Templar, lends weight to the theory. Gothic architecture, including the magnificent cathedrals involved, began to flourish at the same time. St Bernard was known to have admired Druidic knowledge and Celtic lore, e.g. his friendship with Malachie of Ireland. Rigby states:

*'Since the emplacement of monasteries established after St Robert's death were linked closely to the pattern of the*

*pentagram held by the Plough, we must assume that if Robert was the source of knowledge regarding the ground pattern, he had passed much of what he knew to someone else before he died – the two most likely candidates for this information were Hugues de Champagne (Knights Templar) and Etienne Harding, Abbot of Cîteaux. A third, but less likely possibility, is St Bernard de Clairvaux. But this knowledge could well have been 'passed down the line".'*

The only other possibility for the source of the 'sacred' information, according to Rigby, was in the House of Tonnerre, and more precisely it reposed in the Monastery of St Michel de Tonnerre, established in the sixth century and one of the oldest monasteries in France. But St Robert was Abbot of this monastery from 1068 until 1071. So the information was used again by Robert.

### The crucial lateral leap

Nowhere in his book does Rigby mention St Bruno, but the link now seemed so clear to me and answered the fundamental question. If there existed one system linking the Great Bear and the pentagram in northern France, why should there not be another similar one elsewhere? If St Robert was the 'keeper' of this knowledge, then he could have had the opportunity to discuss and pass on the location to St Bruno, when the latter stayed at Sèche-Fontaine. Ravier states that the reason why St Bruno came to Grenoble is unknown. My assertion is this: he decided to found a settlement in a forsaken wilderness that St Robert knew had a similar, but much smaller, configuration to the one he knew of in northern France. St Robert was tied to Molesmes, but Bruno was on his way to find a hermit's peace, in the most fitting place.

The only alternative is that either Bruno knew already the information or it was Seguin who passed it on to Hugues, and possibly to Bruno. But Bruno still had to link up with Hugues. Seeing that there is so much uncertainty about possible liaisons between these three, the undisputed fact that Bruno spent time with Robert points heavily towards my main assertion that St Robert was the main instigator.

The way in which it has been reported down the centuries that Hugues' dream of seven stars was linked to Bruno's arrival with six companions appears to be a way of concealing the real explanation behind a smokescreen. Yet St Hugues knew the region as well as anyone. Indeed it must be remembered that these men were very learned. St Robert founded Molesmes in 1075; Seguin was in charge at la Chaise-Dieu between 1078 and 1094; St Bruno left Reims at some time between 1081–3; Bruno and Robert were practically the same age, by all accounts, and were always very friendly to each other; Hugues was the youngest. The links between them might not have been quite so tenuous as previously thought; and Rigby's book provided the breakthrough to find the combination.

### *The search for the 'way' of the Plough*

The last main step seemed at first to be simple. Just superimpose the Plough and the elongated sides of the 'bowl' around the pentagram and everything would fall into place, but it proved rather different!

Firstly, expanding the outline of the Plough to the right proportions was finicky using straightforward ratio multiplication and trying to get the angles correct. But perseverance won the day and I aligned the formation around the pentagram. But the star pattern did not fit any worthwhile points – I was close to despair! Was all my careful research going to fail at the last hurdle, after all? The 'handle' of the Plough did lead towards Grenoble, but it did not reveal any notable sites coincidental with the stars in the formation.

So, using the *same* correctly-proportioned expanded Plough plan, I looked independently of the pentagram. Suddenly, four points coincided!

St Hugues, along with St Bruno's group, had set out from Grenoble, passed through Corenc, the Col de Vence [see

**Plate 13: The Col de Vence, marked out by the second star of the Plough's handle (Mizar).**

plate 13], le Sappey [see plate 14 page 43] and the Col de Palaquit before arriving at the Col de Porte. From there they descended towards St Pierre de Chartreuse, before bearing west through the Porte de l'Enclos and then north to the actual site.

I had *four points* coinciding with the route taken: **Grenoble, the Col de Vence, the church at le Sappey** and **the Col de Porte** [see plate 15]. *Two other points* on my tracing coincided with *two cols:* that of **Mauvernay,** just below the summit of the Grand Som to the north-west; and that of **l'Aliénard,** a bit further to the north-west [see figure 13]. These two cols are equidistant from and on opposite sides of where St Bruno sited his first settlement. It then struck me that cols would be of far more use as a guide to travellers once in the actual area than mountain peaks, and two marked the furthest points of the journey. So the **Col de Mauvernay** [plate 16] is important on my map of the Plough. Ravier, while talking about the springs near the site established by St Bruno, mentions this same name. He says:

# Part Four: The Crucial Link

The route highlighted by the 'Plough'

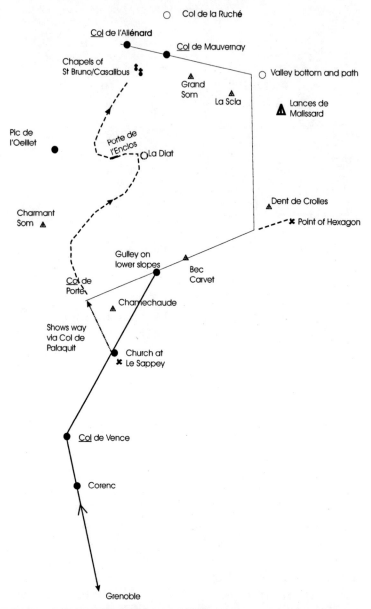

**Figure 13: The route taken by St Bruno and St Hugues to go into the Chartreuse, as shown by the Plough (on the same scale as the pentagram in figure 9).**

**Plate 15: The route towards le col de Porte from le Sappey en Chartreuse, from the same viewpoint.**

*'But Bruno found many other springs, and more plentiful ones, in the valley, for example, the delightful and swollen Mauvernay spring, which Guigues decided upon in choosing the site of the present monastery.'*

Other interesting factors also appeared:

- Joining the third star/point along the 'handle' to the elongated line of the 'inner bowl' follows the path taken by Hugues and Bruno via the Col de Palaquit and the resultant triangle encapsulates Chamechaude.
- The Bec Charvet lies halfway along the short ' bowl' line, which, if extended, meets the south-east point of the original Seal of Solomon.
- The bottom 'bowl' line fringes the Dent de Crolles and the Lances de Malissard before showing the line of the valley between la Scia and the latter. Then the outer extended 'bowl' line leads to the two aforementioned cols.
- The route taken from the Col de Porte to the settlement falls within the 'bowl' of the Plough, with la Diat, the original centre of St Pierre de Chartreuse, almost in the middle of it.

**Plate 16: The present monastery from the Grand Som. From the same standpoint, the present monastery is visible. The Col de Mauvernay is just to the right.**

All in all, the top section of the star formation provides the major route taken and the 'bowl' delineates the major amphitheatre effect of the original mountain layout.

This star map would indeed have shown Hugues and Bruno the way and given a good indication of the stages on the journey. With six out of nine points hitting precise targets, and with these showing the most important stages of the journey, I felt that my confidence in thinking laterally was rewarded [see figure 13].

## In the reverse direction

I knew that the 'dream' had a practical explanation that now linked it inextricably with Grenoble. What if the star pattern map could provide a pointer back towards the Cluse de Chambéry to the north?

Accordingly, I reset the Plough tracing – but this time around the pentagram – and found that, with the 'handle' pointing north-east, its last two stars fell either side of the ridge between the Pointe de la Bornée and Mt Joigny. What could be made of this interesting placement? The idea came to me to extend the line beyond the last two stars and I realised it was pointing back to Mt St Michel across the Cluse de Chambéry. This was final confirmation that the Plough had a dual role to play: showing the Chartreux site from both south and north directions – and leading me back to my departure point across the whole valley.

When I did the circular walk from the Col de Granier to Mt Joigny and back, the confirmation of all the map work and its resultant discovery in this direction became abundantly clear, in that Chamechaude was indeed the pivotal point. For from where the line between the last two stars cross the ridge (in fact more easily visible from the path below) Chamechaude rises up magnificently in the distance, but perfectly outlined in the 'V' of the Col de Cucheron to the east of the Grand Som. A pyramid rising directly above the 'V'. *The alignment was perfect to seal this whole 'circular' process.It seemed as if I was back where I had started.*

## The centre of the pentagram

Wondering if the pentagram centre would hold any evidence supporting my hypothesis that the geometry was coaxed out by human endeavour, I went to find it while accompanied by my stalwart friend, Aimé Faucher. The ONF had been making inroads into this rather remote area, which both hindered and helped with some large tractor routes cutting into the route. However, at the correct site, we suddenly came across a flattened clearing in the wood (not due to the ONF) which Aimé, drawing upon his experience as a history/geography teacher, was reasonably sure was a result of some kind of dwelling in the past [see plate 17]. Just down to the side was a large pool which was due to the ONF work, but which had as its source a spring mentioned on the map. This certainly was a contrast to the immediate area around, which consisted of hillocks and tangled undergrowth; but the path we were following was situated in the valley leading up to the Col des Aures and would therefore have been accessible in times gone by.

I had taken as granted that the geometric shapes in the landscape had been fashioned by the Celts and Druids. Therefore the centre of the pentagram would have had some significance as a holy Druidic site, as the amount of effort and skill involved in establishing it would have been enormous.

My reading into Celtic/Druidic holy sites had told me that they were characterised by certain trees, streams and stones. I had here hints of some dwelling-place in a remote

**Plate 17: The clearing in the centre of the pentagram, looking north towards the Col des Aures and the Grand Som.**

wooded area alongside a spring or stream. During one of the lectures, Henry Lincoln asked me if there was a meeting of paths at this very spot, as this was a frequent characteristic, apparently, of Celtic holy places. I struggled to remember exactly, but on reflection I do seem to remember a more indistinct path joining the main one we were on, slightly lower down. I was getting echoes and hints of history in the right spot, in an unfrequented site, but without definite proof.

To reach the Col des Aures by mounting the V-shaped valley towards the south was a real struggle as the path appeared to peter out. Only on our descent later did we manage to locate the overgrown path, which confirmed my belief that this was an ideal place to position the centre of the pentagram. It would certainly have had some mystical aura way back in the past as the enormous bulk of the Dent de L'Ours and the Grand Som reared up directly opposite the path.

Would St Hugues and St Bruno have deliberately followed a trail of holy Celtic sites to establish this new order? The problem is that very little research is obviously available, as this area was on the periphery of the main transport routes of antiquity (and therefore of greater interest) which would have followed the major valleys of the Alps. This was the conclusion of M. Cérino of the Antiquarian Bookshop in the Rue de Boigne in Chambéry, who could not refer me to any published books on the subject, apart from a map of the previous century which unfortunately could not further my investigation. I contacted Dr Karen Ralls-MacLeod, author of *The Celtic Otherworld* and co-author of *The Quest for the Celtic Key* in case she had any information on this area, knowing, however, that her main interest lay in Scottish history. Again I drew a blank, although her reply did reinforce a few aspects of my research. Frustratingly, I could not find any corroboratory evidence, but then my research took an unexpected turn.

# SECTION TWO

# PART ONE: THE GEOMETRY EXPANDS WITH OTHER AGENCIES

## *The Pole Star Connection*

It was a chance comment at the end of my second lecture to the Saunière Society at Conway Hall in London about my previous research that set me off on further discoveries: 'What about the Pole Star, relative to your Plough? You might find a church dedicated to Mary Magdalene!' In fact, I had not got round to thinking along these lines as yet, but it was a valid point.

As my final diagram explaining St Bruno's journey up into the Chartreuse had the handle of the Plough in a north-south direction, with the consequence that the two pointer stars would indicate the Pole Star away to the west, I reverted to the basic, and logical, idea that the Pole Star should at least be in a northern position. The most likely scenario for that would be the first pointer star at Perquelin and the second the stone 'cross' beside the GR9 – in other words, the handle would start in the west. This alignment then lead me across the Cluse de Chambéry into the Massif to its immediate north – the Bauges. Again, the interplay between these two massifs was being re-asserted [see figure 14)].

After much searching on the Internet, I discovered that the Pole Star is situated just about five times the distance between the pointer stars and slightly offset to the east. My curiosity grew with the realisation that the present Chartreuse d'Aillon – a 'satellite' of the main monastery – was in the correct position but very slightly short of the required distance. But on visiting the site, I was informed

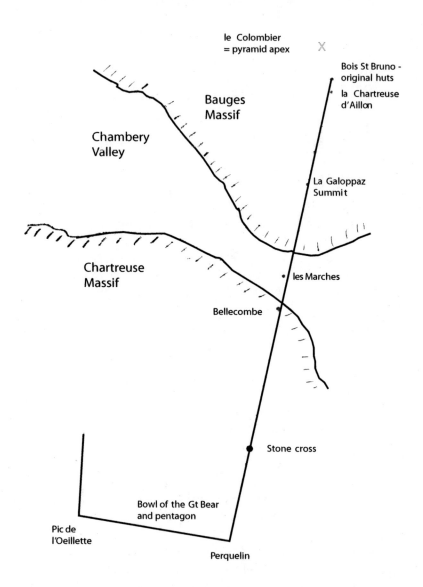

**Figure 14: The Pole Star connection between the bowl of the 'Great Bear' in the Chartreuse and la Chartreuse d'Aillon, next to Aillon-le-Jeune in the Bauges. The apex of the pyramid, le Colombier, is alongside the Pole Star.**

that the initial settlements were further up the high valley, the Combe de Lourdens, alongside the alignment which terminated in the aptly named 'Bois de St Bruno'. The stone ruins of these huts are still extant [see plate 18]. This confirmed my belief that this was no random choice of satellite site.

But a nasty thought struck me almost at once. The stone cross was the last pointer, but it marked the *extended* side of the Plough to coincide with the point of the pentagram and was thus not the real position of the pointer star. However, I reasoned that this could in fact be a salient reason for using it, in that it actually *highlighted the geometry* of the pentagram which was instrumental in the original choice of the settlement. For this reason my initial disquiet was somewhat appeased.

The Chartreuse d'Aillon is situated in a high valley immediately to the east of one of the highest mountains in

**Plate 18: The remains of the original Carthusian dwellings at Aillon-le-Jeune, in the Bauges massif. These are quite a lot higher up the Lourdens valley than the present monastery buildings and mark the position of the Pole Star relative to the Chartreuse 'Plough'.**

**Plate 19: The monastery and the Bois de St Bruno, looking up towards Mt Rochers de la Bade, which continue to Mont Colombier.**

the Bauges, Mt Colombier, which occupies a more central position than its slightly higher neighbours, Mt Arcalod, Mt Pécloz, and Mt Trélod. The alignment falls on its eastern flank and this mountain was to provide another link in my research before too long [see plate 19].

The settlement was founded in 1178 (although some opinion puts the date at 1184) with monks living in huts. The first stone was positioned in 1241 in the presence of Count Amédée IV and donation of land was given by Humbert III, Count of Maurienne and Marquis of Italy. It is interesting at this stage to note that the House of Savoy held the Carthusians in great esteem, as is pointedly mentioned in the official guide book. This would be echoed later on. Several of this establishment's monks and priors came from local seigniories, such as the families of Chignin and Curienne, whose names have both figured earlier in my research.

As this 'satellite' monastery occupies such an important role in relation to the original settlement in the Chartreuse, thereby giving added proof of the latter's deliberate positioning and the Plough, I wondered whether the other two 'satellites' in close proximity were randomly situated, namely la Chartreuse de Curière and St Hugon.

## A *Massive Design*

La Chartreuse de Curière is situated directly south of St Laurent du Pont and directly west of the present monastery, up in a quite secluded spot. It is now in the ownership of the 'Sisters of Bethlehem', but has an official foundation date of 1296, which I considered a little late, taking into account all the activity in setting up these strategically significant settlements of the preceding two centuries. Sure enough, the process of acquiring the property had started in 1129, when the forest of Curière was acquired by the Chartreux and their representative, Othmar de Valbonnais, got possession of the land and buildings off Boniface, the son of Humbert de Miribel. Of significance for me was the fact that St Hugues himself had given final approval shortly before his death a couple of years or so later.

The Chartreuse de St Hugon is in the Bens valley in the foothills of the opposite Belledonne Massif above the village of Arvillard. It is certainly well removed to the north-east of St Bruno's original settlement, on the far side of the huge Isère valley, and I therefore wondered what physical connection it could have to the Chartreuse de Curière. Its name comes from the St Hugues of my research and its construction was started in 1173. Its sumptuous buildings were founded by Hugues d'Arvillard and his wife Audisia and son Hugues. Among a host of other contributors, I was fascinated to discover, were the Templars. This was to figure in my investigation later on when I unexpectedly homed in from another direction. As my startling discovery was to show, there was probably more to St Hugues than a very pious cleric. He was certainly a good administrator and I am sure he had a very positive role in the siting of this establishment away to the north-east which just apparently bears his name.

In the Departmental Archives in Grenoble, I found the original article from the 1866 August edition of *Le Dauphiné* relating the legend of the inauguration ceremony at St Hugon in 1189. It was written down by a certain notary of Allevard named Leverd in 1585 and stated the following vision: a bishop – presumed to be St Hugues – leading a procession of 12 Carthusian monks in white; two bishops at the consecration saw the Holy Oil or Unction come down from on high and anoint the altar without any external assistance. Needless to say, news of this vision spread very rapidly among the nobles and the poor, while the corporal and the altar cloth were kept as mementoes of this divine event.

This was just over 50 years after St Hugues' death and this vision, whether readily recognised as true or not, shows clearly his close association and memory with this precise building which is now a Buddhist centre of learning, the Karma Ling Institute.

My surprise can be imagined when I physically linked up these two properties in the simplest way possible – by drawing a line between them. The line crossed over the summital ridge of the Grand Som very close to the actual summit and *went through the 'stone cross'*.

It was uncanny how this rather insignificant stone with its engraving was being used in this grand design in more ways than one.

A nagging thought was in my mind when I studied the proportions of this 32 km. long line. Could there possibly be a geometric link between the two end points and the stone cross? On careful measuring of both lengths and dividing the shorter into the longer, I arrived at the magical number of 1.6177! This result of finding the Golden Section so accurately was staggering considering the savage landscape [see Addendum 3, page 96]. How on earth could it have been calculated? But this could only mean that there was a huge pentagram – another one! – built into the intricate web I was discovering. My conviction that St Hugues was deeply involved in the setting-up of this proportionate geometry was growing more and more strongly and the fact that the Templars were involved in the founding of St Hugon hinted at a partnership that must have continued after his death in 1132. Hence, perhaps, the accounts of the vision at the inauguration of St Hugon, which is still officially listed among the important dates of its history. St Hugues' name would forever be associated with it in this way.

It was only much later – in the last year of this research – that I found a name given to this stone cross and it was a total vindication, apart from being a great surprise, of my discovery of the alignment between the two, reinforcing its deliberate siting. During a discussion with Aimé and perusing an old 'Topo-Guide' of the Granier-Alpette section of the Chartreuse, dating from 1975, I noticed the small print stating 'croix des Chartreux St Hugon'. Why here at such a distance, and lost from view from St Hugon? The only reason could surely have been to mark the Golden Section property of this alignment. This chance discovery really gave me a massive boost

To avoid any idea of 'fiddling' the result, I asked the Maths/Art departments at my wife's school to construct a pentagram based on my Golden Section find on a 1:50,000 map. Placing the resultant tracing on the map confirmed what I suspected and led me back to where I had started my research [see figure 15]. Henry Lincoln himself thought it would have taken 200 years to measure accurately the basic pentagram with diagonals of 32 km. – a monumental feat. With escarpments, forests and deep valleys all presenting horrendous obstacles, I could only concur, and marvel at the effort involved. But then the timescale of 200 years surely meant that the initial work had been started long before St Hugues' arrival on the scene. The Celts and Druids were coming back into the picture, and the possibility that one group's work was finished by another.

This pentagram could be placed in two ways on the map, depending on the diagonal chosen. However, with the two points in the north, they both overlapped two very important previous sites: Mt St Michel and Mt Grelle. The other point fell on a semi-circular group of hills at the base of the Belledonne chain alongside the Isère valley to the south-east towards Grenoble, at Hurtières. A superb view is apparent towards the north-west, including the escarpment ridge of the eastern Chartreuse and the relatively distant

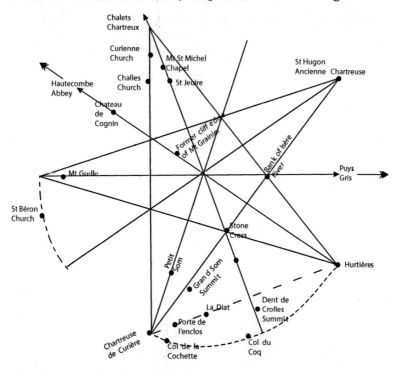

**Figure 15: The vast pentagram stretching from the Chartreuse (bottom left to centre) to the foothills of the Belledonne chain (StHugon) and into the Bauges (top). Key points are indicated. Each diagonal is 32 km. in length.**

Bauges range. Further investigation of this site is required.

Within the north-facing pentagram points, the two central bisecting lines pass through both the original key alignment sites of Mt St Michel and Mt Grelle. St Jeoire is also pinpointed along the former. This could not be another coincidence and served to prove that my original findings were not misguided. The north-west point highlights the area immediately below the south-west corner of lac d'Aiguebelette and leads me to wonder that if the lake was larger in the twelfth century than today, would the point have indicated exactly the limit of the lake at the time? The north-east point's western diagonal passes through, or very close to, the churches of Curienne and Challes-les-Eaux – another echo of previous alignments for Curienne. The line drawn between Curière and Hurtières passes through the Porte de l'Enclos and la Diat, while the bisecting line of the Curière point passes through the summit of the Petit Som. The south-eastern bisecting line goes through the very strategically placed stone cross before hitting the Lances de Malissard and the summital ridge of the Dent de Crolles – all important sites from before.

## The pentagram centre

The centre of the pentagram lies a few hundred yards from the GR9 a short way up the slope leading up from the undulating hollows and hillocks at the back of Mt Granier. It also is on the line between the Col de l'Alpette and the highest trig. point of 1843 m. at the top of the slope, on the ridge between the Rochers de Belles Ombres and the Rochers de l'Alpe. This fact would seem to point to a deliberate siting of the whole structure.

I got as close as I could to where I reckoned the centre to be. I began to struggle as I fought my way around some very difficult terrain to approach it, but then the slope began to aid my progress and I emerged to have a good perspective of the Col de l'Alpette, Mt Pinet, and the cliffs at the rear of Mt Granier. It was the first point to have a clear view when approaching from the Col. It was here that the limestone slabs underfoot ('lapiaz') first began to be evident, with their deep weathered crevasses a real danger for the ankles! [See plate 20.] I could not find one pivotal position that I could point to as indicating any ancient surveying, but the view was the important factor, with a 180° panorama facing me to the west. From further afield, the panorama extends perfectly towards the Bauges.

## A vital alignment from the pentagram

But perhaps the most telling bisecting line of the whole pentagram, when extended outside its immediate peri-

**Plate 20: The distinctive limestone slabs, riven with fissures, which mark this pentagram centre area. The amount of erosion caused by water flowing underground can be imagined.**

meter, is between the two north-facing points. *It passes through the supposed and most likely cliff extension of Mt Granier before the collapse of 1248* – a point arrived at, not just as a result of my own research, but that of Jacques Berlioz as well.

My research was leading me further to the north and around Chambéry itself without seemingly coming into contact with it in any direct way. My instinct told me that such an importantly strategic and historic crossroads must have some connection to all this symbolic geometry. It was to come into closer focus quite soon.

This bisecting line not only passes through Mt Granier's former cliff edge, but also extends directly to the abbey of Hautecombe to which I had referred right at the start of my research, stating that there was a good reason for it being situated where it is – but I was only thinking of its prime lakeside setting opposite Aix-les-Bains. Could this new alignment be pure chance? [See figure 15.] I could perhaps have accepted this argument; however, another possibility suddenly struck me. *On measuring the distance from Hautecombe to Mt Granier's previous cliff extension, I found it to be exactly the same as the pentagram's diagonal.* This discovery served to confirm the pentagram's validity and sent me back to Hautecombe in a search for further clues.

## *The founding of the present Hautecombe*

It had never struck me before as odd that an abbey situated on the lakeside should have the name of Hautecombe, meaning 'high valley'. But the guidebooks dutifully explain that the original abbey had been founded on the other side of the lake, in a high valley near Cessens, in 1101, by Benedictine monks from the Chablais (the Abbey d'Aulps). Then St Bernard of Clairvaux had put forward his reforms and stopping off at Hautecombe on his way to Rome nominated a new abbot who, in 1137, transferred the Cessens community to this new spot donated by the House of Savoy. It was now a Cistercian abbey led by Amédée de Clermont d'Hauterives. The original name was kept. From the twelfth century onwards, the dukes of Savoy have had Hautecombe as their last resting-place.

Other forces were beginning to become apparent in the web: the House of Savoy, St Bernard, and by extension, the Templars, who had already figured in the founding of St Hugon. St Bernard himself had been instrumental in Greg Rigby's research with regard to the moving of Cîteaux and Clairvaux to conform to his pentagram's alignments. Could this move to Hautecombe be another deliberate attempt to fit in with geographical geometry, especially as this particular distance to the visible cliff edge of Mt Granier was equal to the basic pentagram diagonal in the Chartreuse?

Further proof that it was indeed St Bernard himself that chose the site came to light in the foreword to a series of sketches of the cliff-line of Mt Revard, behind Aix-les-Bains, by Abbé Bernard Secret *Le Mont Revard*:

## Part One: The Geometry Expands with other Agencies

*'from the lake will rise up the latin harmonies and the first French murmurings of St Bernard, who chose the site of Hautecombe'* [my rendering].

So, who was party to this geometric knowledge? Was it the monastic Orders, along with the Templars in their infancy, or were they continuing the groundwork of Celtic/Druidic research?

# PART TWO: THE THICKENING OF THE PLOT

## Enter the Cistercians and Templars

As soon as the name of St Bernard of Clairvaux came into the equation, I had the impression that a kind of circle was being completed, especially as he was instrumental in the deliberate choosing of the site of Hautecombe. Let us not forget that it was St Robert of Molesmes who had spent about three years alongside St Bruno before the latter had continued south-east to set up his huts in the Chartreuse with the help of St Hugues. St Robert's successor was Etienne Harding who was known to be well versed in Druidic lore. His successor was St Bernard who turned out to be one of the most charismatic and powerful people of his century and whose life was inextricably linked to the rise of the Templars. In the French periodical, *Les Grands Mystères de l'Histoire*, the following is said about this sometimes shadowy character:

> *'he was probably one of the last highly-placed ecclesiastical figures to have been initiated in Druidic lore (considered at that time to be an heretical movement) by the no less famous Irish monk, Malachie. The latter came to die in his arms, which represents much more than just a simple sign of friendship! Bernard was a learned scholar and a real genius of his time. In keeping with the manner in which he had been taught at Cîteaux, he studied shrewdly, and with insight, all religious cultures and holy texts, even those banned by the Church of Rome. He gathered around him the best translators, as Etienne Harding had done before him, and thus gained access to texts of the great Greek thinkers, to Hebrew and Arabic*

83

*writings, including the Koran and the Cabbale, which
were practically unknown at the time in Europe.'*

Then he chooses the site of Hautecombe which is linked
geometrically to the Chartreuse. Far to the south-east, in
the foothills of the Belledonne Chain, the Templars were
part benefactors of a monastery which bears the name and
memory of St Hugues of Grenoble and which is the major
pivot of a huge pentagram constructed over the Chartreuse
and beyond. And what was in the middle, between the
Chartreuse, the Bauges and Hautecombe? – Chambéry.
There had to be a link, as it was to be the capital of Savoy,
presided over by the House of Savoy, who had granted the
land at Hautecombe and whose family members were to be
buried there from the twelfth century onwards. They also
later granted land in the Bugey to the Chartreux, namely
the château of Pierre-Châtel on the right bank of the river
Rhône, built from the twelfth century and handed over in
1383. My thoughts were turning towards the one historically
verified thing that singled out Chambéry from other Alpine
cities with regard to religious relics – the Holy Shroud. Was
this a flight of fancy, or not, as it would seem at first sight
to be of peripheral relevance? This connection was to return
later.

The concurrent burgeonings of the Cistercian, Templar
and Carthusian Orders seemed to be closely linked,
although not all major developments were in the same
restricted region. However, the Archives in Grenoble do
have documents itemising sales of land between the
Chartreux and the Cistercians in this area. Guigues (the
fifth Prior of the Chartreux) is recorded writing to Hugues
de Payen (the leading founder member of the Templars)
expressing his reservations about their brutal methods
employed in suppressing the infidels in the Holy Land. St
Bernard also visited Guigues in the Chartreuse.

I tried to establish a date list for these organisations
which gave the following results:

| Date | Cistercian/Templar | Carthusian |
|------|--------------------|-----------|
| 1075 | Molesmes founded | |
| 1084 | | St Bruno settles in Chartreuse |
| 1086 | Etienne Harding joins Molesmes | |
| 1098 | Cîteaux founded | |
| 1101 | Cîteaux moved/Hautecombe founded (original abbey) | Death of St Bruno |
| 1106 | | Guigues joins Chartreuse |
| 1109 | Harding becomes Abbot of Cîteaux | Guigues becomes fifth Prior |
| 1112 | St Bernard joins Cîteaux | |
| 1115 | Death of St Robert/Clairvaux founded/St Bernard becomes Abbot of Clairvaux | |
| 1118 | Templars founded | |
| 1127 | Templars returned from Jerusalem | |
| 1128 | Templars officially recognised/ Council of Troyes | |
| 1129 | | La Curière bought in Chartreuse |
| 1132 | | Death of St Hugues of Grenoble |
| 1134 | Death of Etienne Harding | |
| 1135 | Clairvaux moved | |
| 1136 | | Death of Guigues |
| 1137 | Hautecombe Abbey moved to lakeside | |
| 1153 | Death of St Bernard of Clairvaux | |
| 1173 | | St Hugon founded with Templar aid |
| 1178 | | La Chartreuse d'Aillon founded |

These one hundred years certainly seem to have witnessed the explosive growth of the Cistercian Order and the Templars, while the Carthusians continued their steady progression from small beginnings. The major players had their heyday at the same time and their efforts were linked to the landscape here to maintain the memory of something important, otherwise why expend so much effort and time in setting up the geometry? This list certainly fired the interest of Dr Gordon Strachan, a lecturer at Edinburgh University and acclaimed author, at a symposium of the Saunière Society at Newbattle Abbey, as it provided confirmation of his contention that this epoque saw a sudden renaissance of knowledge in Europe and signalled a new age of spiritual advancement.

Under Guigues, another seven 'satellites' were founded, but their sites are generally too far removed to be involved in this precise geometry. In *Les Ordres Religieux – la vie et l'art, Tome 1*, the major ones are:

- la Chartreuse de Portes, near Ambronay, in the Bugey (1115);
- Meyriat, near Nantua, in the Bugey (1116);
- Arvières, in the Bugey, which adopted the basic rules of Carthusian life in 1132;
- Mt Dieu; les Ecouges, in the diocese of Grenoble;
- Durbon, in the Hautes-Alpes;
- Sylve-Bénite in the Vienne diocese.

# PART THREE: THE MARY MAGDALENE CONNECTION

## Linked echoes of Saunière, the Chartreux and St Hugues

So I have other groups entering the question and a definite interplay between them and the Chartreux: the Cistercians, the Templars and the House of Savoy. The pentagram was still unexplained as to its precise symbolic meaning here in the mountains.

However, I found that it was meant also, via the analogy with Venus, to represent **Mary Magdalene** through her love for Jesus. Could the five-pointed symbolism of two and three – the female and male numbers – combining together in marriage represent the supposed union of her and Jesus? Such a monumental task undertaken in the landscape could be warranted by such a statement, but it was one which could hardly have been looked upon favourably by the Church. And the statement would be there for ever for those who knew where and how to look. Could the Carthusians have been a party to such occult knowledge or perceived heresy? Such innovatory and disturbing thoughts troubled me until I read André Douzet's book, translated as *Saunière's Model and the Secret of Rennes-le-Château.*

In it, Douzet includes instances of how Bérenger Saunière, parish priest of Rennes-le-Château in the very early 1900s, came into contact with the Carthusians, especially in the course of his research into Mary Magdalene in France. I had the distinct feeling that I was returning to my source of inspiration of many years before, Rennes-le-Château and Henry Lincoln. But Mary Magdalene was one of the primordial figures in the story and her links with

France needed exploring, especially now that the Carthusians were being linked to her.

My enquiries had previously centred on the well-known stories of her arriving at Ste Marie-de-la-Mer in Provence with companions shortly after the Crucifixion. Her reclusive years at Ste Baume in a cave, and the struggle between Vézelay and St Maximin for the official recognition of having her relics, are well documented. So is the theme of the *The Holy Blood and the Holy Grail* by Lincoln, Baigent and Leigh who follow the bloodline of the sacred couple, Jesus and Mary, into the lineage of the French Merovingian kings and into the mysterious world of secret societies, primarily the 'Prieuré de Sion'. Their book follows the path of the enigmatic priest of Rennes-le-Château, Bérenger Saunière, and his great interest in this particular religious icon.

According to André Douzet, there are other clear links between the Carthusians and Mary Magdalene. The major one concerns the **Roussillon family**, starting with Gérard de Roussillon, who founded Vézelay. At his request, the Burgundian monks claimed they transferred Mary's body to Vézelay from Provence at the time when the Moors occupied the region and threatened to pillage the tomb. However, in Provence, Prince Charles de Salerne undertook a dig in the crypt of St Maximin in 1279 to disprove their claims. This was after the visit of 'Saint' Louis [see Addendum 2] to Aix-en-Provence to honour Mary Magdalene in 1254.

Gérard opposed the king, Charles the Bald, in 870, left Vienne (Isère) and took refuge in a nearby fortress, probably in the Pilat region, east of St Etienne and south-west of Lyons. He eventually surrendered and went into exile. In the eleventh century, the Roussillons appeared in the Pilat and being supporters of the Magdalene cult, built a chapel dedicated to her and belonging to their fief of **Châteauneuf**, near Rive de Guier. It was said to possess relics of St Lazarus, Mary's brother.

In the thirteenth century, the lord of Châteauneuf, Guillaume de Roussillon, died defending St Jean d'Acre. His widow, Béatrix, abandoned Châteauneuf and followed the example of Mary; she supposedly left on horseback, and following a vision of a luminous cross surrounded by stars, crossed over mountains until the vision guided her to a place where she founded the Carthusian monastery of Ste Croix-en-Jarez.

This had an unmistakable echo of St Bruno and St Hugues. But Saunière apparently came to this very monastery in search of something important concerning Mary and did not find it, although, allegedly, he was given money by the Carthusian monks. The reason why is not known, but the question remains: did Guillaume de Roussillon leave some material concerning Mary with his wife who then passed it on to the Carthusian monks at this monastery?

Douzet states that it is really to the Bishopric of Marseilles that we need to look for traces of Mary. Her cave is in this bishopric, near the Carthusian house of Montrieux, founded, interestingly enough, in 1117. The religious services in the cave are still, according to him, maintained by Carthusian monks.

Another possible tantalising link with the Pilat is Lupé castle, dating from the tenth century. It was apparently built in such a way that its battlements and turrets resemble the outline of the Plough; its underground chambers at one time were rumoured to have had some remains of Mary.

What to make of all this circumstantial evidence? There would certainly seem to be a link between the Carthusians and Mary Magdalene, but why would any important material be held secretly in the Pilat and not in the Chartreuse, apart from the strong family connections of the Roussillons?

Surprisingly, there is one single reference to Hautecombe in Douzet's book – that the Roman Prayer Book was drafted by monks there and concludes: 'she became the best friend of her Saviour'. These important connections prompted me to write directly to him. I asked him if there were any other links between Hautecombe and Mary:

- if the fief of Châteauneuf belonging to the Roussillon family was the same as in the title of St Hugues, the

very one who took St Bruno up into the Chartreuse;
- and if he knew of other links between the Carthusians, Saunière and Mary Magdalene.

His reply deepened the mystery. Apparently, there are legends connecting the area around the lac du Bourget with the story of Mary Magdalene, without the link being particular to this spot. I have still to find elucidation on these legends, despite much local research. However, several Cistercian properties are situated in places where the legend of Mary is often found. But she especially is very often represented in the form of statues in the chapels and churches of the Carthusians elsewhere in France as well.

He did not think that the fief of Châteauneuf referred to in the Roussillon family name was the same *geographically*. The Châteauneuf of St Hugues' title is 'sur Isère', just to the north-east of Valence, downriver from Grenoble. However, the *lineage* was from the same family root. Many family members joined the Carthusians, taking key posts in this area of the Rhône-Alpes and at Ste Croix-en-Jarez in particular.

Other links between Mary, Saunière and the Carthusians were, according to him, at Maguelonne, Bonpas and Ballaruc.

So I was more convinced now that there were definite links between Mary Magdalene and the Carthusians, especially through the Châteauneuf connection:

- the founding of Ste Croix-en-Jarez was strangely reminiscent of St Bruno's journey;
- the Cistercian link with Mary (or at least her image) was echoed by apparently not well-known legends about her and the area of the lac du Bourget and possibly Hautecombe itself;
- that establishment would have been pivotal to the area at that time. There were quite close links between the Carthusians and the Cistercians, and, by extension, presumably, a Templar influence, in the area around the Chartreuse and the Bauges in the twelfth century.

It was time to turn my attention back towards that distance equivalent to the 'Golden Section' pentagram measurement from Hautecombe to the previous cliff edge of Mt Granier.

### A flat representation of the Great Pyramid – in Savoy!

I was at first tempted to fit together two pentagrams side by side and partly interlocking until I realised the logistical nightmare of such a huge undertaking, and the amount of time it would have warranted, to survey such a vast area. In addition, the land quickly becomes much flatter to the west of this most southern spur of the Jura, the Mt de la Charve and the Mt du Chat. Surely there had to be a simpler answer. And would not a connection with Chambéry itself, fitting in with the geographical geometry, be a logical result?

However, try as I might, the next piece of the jig-saw was proving very elusive. A suggestion came, at a symposium, to read the book by David Furlong *The Keys to the Temple: unravel the mysteries of the Ancient World.* I was surprised to learn that the Great Pyramid exhibits a Golden Mean proportion between half the base and the slope. Here, in Savoy, I had a line which, for some reason, was equal in length to the pentagram diagonal across the Chartreuse (which had an inherent Golden Mean), and was, in addition, part of the peripheral structure connected to the pentagram, although there was no other apparent spot along the line to provide the corresponding proportion.

On dividing the line between Hautecombe and Mt Granier in half, I followed the 'height' line of the Pyramid east towards the Bauges. My curiosity was aroused when it cut the summital ridge of the previously mentioned Mt Margeriaz in half, before arriving precisely at the summit of Mt Colombier, which overlooks, on its eastern flank, the very Carthusian satellite settlement at Aillon-le-Jeune which served as the 'Pole Star' marker for the original Chartreuse pentagram. Here was a definite link-up, . . . and another pure coincidence?

I constructed the pyramid [see figure 16] and calculated

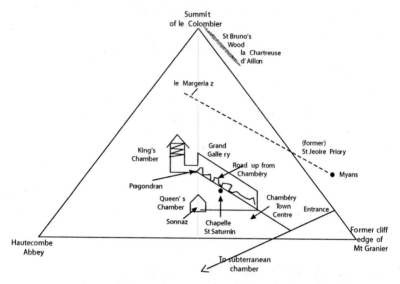

Pyramid, showing main points, including first main alignment
between Mt Margeriaz and Myans

**Figure 16: The major points of the Pyramid, formed by
Hautecombe Abbey, the previous cliff-edge of Mt Granier (at
best independent estimations) and Mt Colombier; the latter
is alongside the representation of the Pole Star position
from the original pentagram in the Chartreuse. Beneath the
entrance corridor to the King's Chamber is Pragondran and
under the Queen's Chamber is Sonnaz. The first major
alignment of the whole research between Myans and le
Margeriaz is shown, which passes through the key point of
the former Priory of St Jeoire.**

the proportion to be slightly less than the exact one I was
hoping for, by about 0.05: not bad at all, I considered, when
my old-fashioned technical drawing methods are taken into
account. The angle of the slope was just over 51°, which is
very close to the optimum. The side of the pyramid from the
former clifftop of Mt Granier cut through the position of the
former priory of St Jeoire (now non-existent, but next to the
present one) on its way up to Mt Colombier, which struck a
chord with the main alignment across the Cluse of

Chambéry that I had found right back at the start of my research. Was this a deliberate ploy to link up with the Chambéry valley? I was further intrigued to find that the two resultant distances on this 'slope', provided by the position of St Jeoire, gave me a very close reading to another instance of the Golden Section, 1.698. A very near miss . . . or a coincidence?

The thought then struck me that not many of the learned elite in the twelfth century or thereabouts would have had the knowledge of the Great Pyramid or its dimensions, so who could have been responsible for its measurement over the landscape, and on the horizontal plane? Taking the view that Hautecombe is Cistercian and that they had close ties with the Templars, it was becoming highly likely that the latter were essential to its construction.

I contacted Jim Munro, a Senior Freemason and vastly experienced guide to Rosslyn Chapel, to ask if the Templars would have known all about the Great Pyramid on their return from their initial sorties to the Holy Land.

Rosslyn Chapel stands just over seven miles from Edinburgh in a small village of the same name. Construction was started in 1446 at the behest of Sir William St Clair, a hereditary Grand Master of the Scottish Masons, and halted about 40 years later. The chapel is filled with stone codes, symbols, alphabets and imagery that are a testament to Freemasonry and Templar traditions, among others. Much still defies full explanation and there is a recent groundswell of opinion that the Templar treasure is buried in inaccessible vaults beneath the chapel.

Munro was sure that they would have, through their contacts with the Islamic world . . . and not only that, but the internal chambers and galleries as well. The Great Pyramid, constructed according to the Golden Section, would be part of this secret knowledge. This was vital confirmation which allayed my fears that I was including an alien symbol in my investigation.

This certainly began to answer my queries as to why a pyramid should be drawn over the landscape here. The thought occurred to me that someone standing on the previous extremity of the cliff edge of Mt Granier would have seen the salient silhouette of the pyramid of Chamechaude to the south, Chamechaude, the key-stone to the Seal of Solomon around St Pierre de Chartreuse. What could be more natural than to recreate the same shape to the north, starting from the same spot, but on a horizontal plane! But then no one could have foreseen the catastrophic collapse of that very part of Mt Granier which formed the right-hand base corner of the geometric design. It would be natural to suppose that the loss of this cornerstone blurred the memory of the design.

# PART FOUR: THE MEDIEVAL BACK IN THE FRAM.

## Further historical impetus and expansion from sources in France

I was very pleasantly surprised to discover that new possible linked areas for research were being suggested by some French journals, which tied in with the direction towards which I now found myself being drawn. Mainstream French research seemed to be mostly orientated towards the accepted Catholic wisdom, but the mould has recently started to change, with fascinating questions surfacing.

When I found that the Cathars were being mentioned in the same breath as the Templars and Ancient Egypt, along with Saunière and Rennes-le-Château, the scope of the questions asked seemed like ever-widening ripples. Yet it was very reassuring.

On perusing *Les Grands Mystères de l'Histoire – L'Hérésie Cathare (hors-série)*, I was fascinated to discover on page 95 that some very similar questions to my own were being posed, namely:

- would the Templars have been in possession of the secrets of Ancient Egypt relating to the treasure of Solomon's Temple?
- would the Cathars have had the same knowledge?
- would Bérenger Saunière of Rennes-le-Château have discovered some of these secrets?

This same publication makes the connection that the early lords of the Languedoc, who most probably supported the Cathars, were very likely to be descended from the Visigoths. These invaders, originally from the Baltic, overcame Greece in the fourth century before sacking Rome in 410AD. under Alaric. They moved on to the south of France where they made Toulouse their capital. They embraced Christianity but abandoned it for a dualist doctrine similar to that of the Cathars, namely, Arianism, which was considered a heresy, especially so after the Council of Nicea in 325AD. Arianism held that Christ was inferior to the Father, was a created being that came into existence at God's behest, thereby unable to share His divinity. The Nicene Creed became the statement of Church orthodoxy and a rejection of Arianism. The Visigoths were also said to have had with them the treasures of Rome, including, possibly, some of the treasures that Rome had gained from its sacking of Jerusalem. This is where another great controversy rears its head – namely, was the treasure still hidden under the Temple Mount or had it (even in part) been discovered by the Romans and transported to Rome?

This period of prosperity could not last. The Francs under Clovis arrived in 507AD supported by the Catholic Church to fight against this doctrine of Arianism. The Visigoths were defeated by Clovis and withdrew to Spain. Yet they still had under their control a little village in the Aude – Rhedae, namely, Rennes-le-Château. The Visigoths were again defeated by the Moors in the eighth century, but allied themselves through marriage to their victors. A part of their treasure was hidden not far from Montségur. This could be the mooted famous discovery by Saunière at Rennes-le-Château.

Some treasure could have come equally from the Merovingians, whose last monarchs were devoid of any power in 680AD. Under Pépin II, they were preparing a 'coup d'état' to regain real influence and the throne, but the Visigoths pre-empted the strike by removing Sigebert, the next in line, and bringing him to Rennes-le-Château. They made an alliance in 681AD. Sigebert's son, in 757AD, decided to replace him on the throne, but left the region with a part of the Merovingian treasure. However, he left another part, consigned to the care of the Blanchefort family, who would keep it in safe hands for his descendants. It is interesting to note that the last inheritor of the Blanchefort family – and therefore of the treasure – is Bernard de Blanchefort, who turns out to be the Templar Grand Master between 1156 and 1169.

When the Cathars were expelled from Montségur, the Templars did not pursue their remnants. This might seem rather odd, as the Templars were supposed to obey the Pope in every respect. They would have been perfect allies for the Crusaders against the Cathars, since their commanderies would have been suitable staging-posts, their intimate knowledge of the terrain would have been invaluable for these 'foreign' northern knights, and their valour in battle was legendary. Yet the Templars took no part in any military operation against the Cathars. There are a few possible reasons for this:

- their commanderies were just agricultural concerns, providing revenues for the real Crusaders in the Holy Land and their numbers were limited in each commandery;
- they maintained close links with the local minor nobility, who helped the Cathars, as they provided vital donations to the Order and many had indeed joined the Templars – so were they going to fight against close family members?
- or did they refuse to fight in an unjust war, as St Bernard had exhorted them to have the purest of intentions when fighting for Christ and not to have personal gain as an object?

### Local evidence of Cathar influence

Then, on page 121 of the above publication, which I only discovered long after all the geometrical measurements had been made, a paragraph really set my mind racing.

With regard to the inquisition against the Cathars, the crusaders tried to destroy their symbols and cult objects; yet, traces are still extant, notably, the Pentagon and the Dove, the latter being, in French, 'la colombe'. *The apex of the pyramid is 'le Colombier' (dovecote) and just alongside is la Chartreuse d'Aillon, the symbolic guiding point of the Pole Star*. From one mountain chain to another, the Great Bear in the Chartreuse leads the eyes to the Pole Star in the Bauges. Then the universal guide of the heavens pinpoints the 'Cathar-tipped' apex of the Great Pyramid right alongside. It was as if the next steps were falling into place in a logical order. The white dove, for the Cathars, represented the divine spirit and equally the soul reaching another dimension. What could be more natural than for this symbol to be a *mountain top reaching towards the heavens*?

Jean Markale of the Sorbonne [c.f. select bibliography] states that doves carved in stone as well as ceramic ones have been discovered in the Montségur area – one in Ussat-les-Bains and two at Montségur itself. He links up these finds with the dove mentioned in Wolfram von Eschenbach's Middle Ages Grail text, *Parzival*, the dove that comes every Good Friday to the Holy Grail in its form of a stone, bearing a sacramental host, as well as the depiction of the Holy Ghost in Cathar tradition and the Huguenot cross surmounted by a dove. The dove bringing the olive branch back to Noah in his ark also springs to mind.

Stated there as well is the realisation that the Templar Cross (la Croix Pattée) is in fact simply a flat projection of a pyramid. Needless to say, I felt vindicated and relieved in equal measure; and as the former priory of St Jeoire (St George) lies on the right-hand sloping side of the pyramid, it is doubly interesting here that it was the Templars who used this saint's emblem of a red cross on a white background. Could this be a double concealed hint of their involvement in the vast geometrical design here?

Further investigation of the priory revealed some interesting clues:

- the official guidebook states that the cult of St George probably came into Savoy through the intermediary of an important individual who participated in a crusade. Here again was a direct official link back to the Templars;
- the heraldic shield above the main door [see plate 26]

**Plate 26: The heraldic shield above the main door at St Jeoire Prieuré. Its age is uncertain, but the pentacle is still a recurrent image. No explanation is as yet forthcoming.**

has worn smooth over time, but a definite pentacle is an important part of the decoration. Is this, as suggested earlier with regard to the porches of the chapels on the original sites of St Bruno's settlement in the Chartreuse, purely artistic licence, or is a sub-text being continued over time?

- M.Terreaux, a local expert on the church, whom I contacted for elucidation, was not able to give precise answers to my questions about the Crusader's identity nor the design or date of the shield. He thought the latter was not particularly old, but why then was it so faded?

During my guided visit around the priory, most graciously arranged by M.Ortolland one Sunday morning, I was given a copy of a detailed guide to the building by Marie-Astrid Orth, Patrimoine Médiéval, Histoire de l'art. In her appraisal of the reasons for the priory's founding in this location, there seem to be some uncertainties, apart from the fact of the sometimes stormy relations between the counts of Savoy and the ecclesiastical dignatories, who wished to remain independent:

- she finds it surprising that the bishop of Grenoble should found a priory right in the middle of land owned by the counts of Savoy. She poses the questions as to who was responsible for this project and what were the motivations;
- the lords of the Dauphiné could have pressurised St Hugues into founding the priory so as to weaken their enemies from Savoy;
- the counts of Geneva were powerful lords whose influence was felt in a large part of Savoy. This priory could have been judiciously placed to impress the neighbours;
- or was the priory just part of the twelfth century's period of demographic expansion and economic renewal, where new towns, villages and parishes grew up alongside the expanding monastic communities and the interior of the mountain massifs were accordingly opened up to the benefit of their inhabitants?

In her opinion, these beginnings are still shrouded in doubt. I feel that this adds weight to my conclusions about the geometric basis of its positioning.

I enquired about the particular geographical origin of 'le Colombier' at Aillon-le-Jeune. The former mayor, M.Gaston Trépier, and his family welcomed me into their house to discuss this local history, but could not say from what date that name existed. He did state that the name Combe de Lourdens, on the other side of the Colombier, where the Chartreux founded their settlement, was based on 'ours', namely, 'bear', which was quite probably a straightforward explanation, taking into consideration the prevalent wild animals of the time. But the link (fortuitous?) with Bruno, the Great Bear constellation and here the Pole Star equivalent was not lost on me.

In response to further probing, via the Chambéry Departmental Archives, the Musée Savoisien did tell me that they had a map of the region dating from the fifteenth century that had 'le Colombier' on it. So is it beyond the realms of possibility that the name was accorded in the thirteenth century with a specific reason in mind, that it should symbolically record the advent of the Cathar treasure and point to its location? Now that the Cathars were definitely 'in the frame', a closer look at this pyramid was required.

### Surprises within the Pyramid

This sent me back to trace out the positions of the Queen's and King's Chambers over the map, and the result confirmed my suspicions [see figure 16].

Just as David Furlong had discovered a Templar establishment in the King's Chamber position in his discoveries in the English Downs, there is a village/hamlet in each Chamber position here: Sonnaz in the Queen's, and Pragondran in the King's. Pragondran is the highest hamlet below the western summital ridge of Mt Nivolet overlooking Chambéry and the road ends here in a kind of bowl. Actually, to be very precise, the tiny hamlet of Pragondran lies just where the Grand Gallery passes into the entrance corridor before the chamber. The centre of the Chamber is at the northern end of the bowl at a spot called Malpassant – a sort of small col.

Furthermore, the only road which tightly meanders up to Pragondran *follows the outline of the Grand Gallery* and leads up from the higher central part of present Chambéry [see plate 22]. The bottom of the Gallery extends down to just below the river Leysse, to the immediate east of the centre. Given that the land in the valley was swampy centuries ago and the major paths of communication between Lyon and Italy, Grenoble and Aix-le-Bains followed this side of the valley – passing through Lemencum, the site of the present Lémenc and its famous crypt – I could now see the link with Chambéry that I had been seeking.

But could the point of all this land surveying work be just to conceal something? I turned back to Furlong and was interested to learn that, in short, defunct objects placed within a pyramid show a slower rate of decomposition or an

**Plate 22: The view down the road from Vérel, with its church in its prominent position, following the Grand Gallery outline. Mt Granier can be distinguished in the background.**

enhanced time of effectiveness. The theory is that the shape of the pyramid interacts with the Earth's magnetic current, producing 'electromagnetic dehydration': i.e. energy produced by the pyramid removes molecules of water in/on the object, thereby reducing the speed of decomposition, and prolonging its effectiveness. There is a vast amount of anecdotal evidence also to support the view that pyramid energies can have beneficial healing effects.

Could the Templars – if they were the prime movers in this construction – with, presumably, the tacit support of the Cathars, have wanted to preserve something precious in a symbolic or metaphorical sense, as this is only a flat representation of one side of the Pyramid? If so, they would surely have put it in the symbolic location of the King's and/

or the Queen's Chamber? This object or repository of knowledge would have to be very important to justify the huge effort put into its location by linking it to the huge pentagram across the Chartreuse and the Bauges. Then there is the fact that the entrance to this 'chamber' leads up from Chambéry along the outline of the Grand Gallery. The overriding link still seemed to go back to Mary Magdalene and her links to both the Cathars and the Templars.

I contacted M.Yves Cérino again in Chambéry to enquire about any legends connecting Marie Magdalene to the area around the lac du Bourget or near the Chartreuse, any Templar influences near Chambéry, the latter's population spread in the twelfth century, and whether anything extraordinary was connected to the higher ground near Chambéry overlooking the lake. While awaiting a reply, from which no enlightening information proceeded, the net widened as I pondered on the other mystery which had involved Chambéry and, in a broader sense, Savoy – the Holy Shroud. Although this would appear to be going off on a tangent, this tremendously important religious artefact linked strongly to Chambéry with possible Templar connections needed some investigation to see if it was related to my own research.

# PART FIVE: FURTHER BACK IN TIME

## The Holy Shroud, the House of Savoy and the Templar links

Ever since my first year spent in Chambéry in 1970–71 and on numerous occasions since, I have visited the Sainte Chapelle in the Château and been struck by its part in the history of the Shroud (and equally by the 'trompe l'oeil' effect of the ceiling which, although painted, gives the impression of stonework in relief). There is a detailed family tree of the House of Savoy in the little museum next door, but I had never really thought much about it until my research got to this point.

When the carbon-dating of the Shroud 'proved' it to be a medieval item, I was fascinated by the books which appeared about it. The one which I now came back to because of its direct relevance to my main thrust of enquiry – Carthusians, Templars, (and by extension, Freemasonry), Cistercians, and the House of Savoy – was by Christopher Knight and Robert Lomas *The Second Messiah*.

Details which I had glossed over before and forgotten now stood out as important clues for my own quest. The authors had asked themselves the very same questions, which recently occurred to me quite independently and which I was excited to rediscover in their book, about, specifically, the Shroud and the House of Savoy.

The main point of this, their second book on this theme of the origins of Freemasonry, maintains that the image on the Shroud is that of the last Grand Master of the Templars, Jacques de Molay, who was crucified before being burnt at the stake in Paris in 1314, along with Geoffrey de Charney.

The Shroud resurfaces in Lirey to be exhibited in 1357 by later generations of the de Charney family before being sold or passed on for safer keeping to Louis, the second Duke of the House of Savoy, their distant relations, in 1453. Louis gave two castles in return for the Shroud whose provenance had been the source of much acrimonious debate between Bishop Pierre d'Arcis and the Pope, Clement VII, who kept to his first decision that, whenever it was displayed, it should be announced that it was just a 'figure or representation'. It is interesting to note that the lady mainly responsible for displaying the Shroud, Jeanne de Vergy, was, by a fortuitous marriage, the aunt to the Pope!

The contention is that the Church encouraged the worship of such miraculous relics as this, ostensibly from the Resurrection itself, as it strengthened their authority over the people. But if the secret Templar origin of the Shroud came out and was accepted, Jacques de Molay would become a martyr and the Church would suffer huge embarrassment and vilification. The surviving Templars would become the leaders of a cult, threatening the existence of the Church. So, the ecclesiastical authorities not being able to destroy it, they could not admit its true provenance either – and the classic 'fudge' resulted.

The House of Savoy have owned the Shroud ever since and it was housed for almost 80 years over the late fifteenth and early sixteenth centuries in Chambéry before being moved, for its security, around Savoy. Between 1561 and 1578 it was kept in the Sainte Chapelle before its final transfer to Turin Cathedral, where it remains today. Unrecognised by myself for so long previously, when I had read their book for the first time, as a fundamental question now in my research, Lomas and Knight asked themselves if the House of Savoy knew about this origin of the Shroud and, if they did, why did they go along with the lack of clarification?

## *The origins of the House of Savoy*

Firstly, it should be noted that the House of Savoy is one of Europe's oldest dynasties, having ruled over Italy from 1861 till 1946. It was established by Humbert 'the Whitehanded' after devastating Saracen invasions of the first half of the tenth century followed by a long line of inept Frankish/Merovingian kings and then the Rodolphes sovereigns in Savoy. In 1032, the last Rodolphe passed on heirless, so Humbert set the scene for Savoy to become a political power. He was at first a minor lord, probably from the **Burgundian** line which had taken over Savoy between 450 and 536AD. But he was well connected, especially with the German Emperor, and he acquired control over four of the six main Alpine passes while expanding his holdings further west and east. He died around 1048 with the title of Count of Savoy. His successors steadily increased their territory and, in 1232, Chambéry became the capital during the reign of Thomas I, 1189 – 1233. Since those early times, the interworkings of this family with the Papacy, the ecclesiastical authorities and other royal lines are intricate. It is interesting to note that the dates marking the rise in importance of Chambéry coincide with those of the Templars.

It should also be borne in mind that the eleventh and twelfth centuries saw the massive upsurge in religious establishments in this area, especially priories and abbeys in communities around Chambéry and Grenoble. Pertinently for my research, the House of Savoy gave the land for Hautecombe to be resited by the Cistercians in 1137 alongside the lac du Bourget and were founders/benefactors of St Hugon and Aillon, amongst others. Indeed, it was the Carthusians who were doted on first by the family.

Another further and intriguing question posed by Lomas and Knight – that the House of Savoy may well be members of 'Rex Deus' – seemed to be supported by the links with the Cistercians and the Templars, added to the fact of their longevity among Europe's elite. To answer this question, another shadowy and relatively unknown supposed bloodline needs to be explored, that of the Rex Deus families.

## The Rex Deus theory

This title ('King(s) of God') was explained to the above authors by a distinguished and sincere Frenchman who, while wishing to remain anonymous, professed to be a direct descendant of the Templar leader, Hugues de Payen. His father passed on secret knowledge to him when he attained 21 years of age and which he would be beholden to do likewise with his own chosen son. Thus this knowledge was passed on down the generations via this purely oral tradition and had been done so for hundreds of years within his family; the same would have happened in certain other families.

The knowledge, in short, relates how the Nasorene Priesthood of the Temple of Jerusalem had fled just before the sacking of the Temple by the Romans in 70AD. They had hidden their most important artefacts and scrolls beneath the Temple and had passed down knowledge of them to a favourite son over the centuries. This knowledge was said to include, written on the walls of the subterranean chambers, the genealogies of the children of the priests of the Temple descended from the pure lines of Aaron and David right from the birth of the Hebrew nation. They had fled into Europe to be assimilated in the most important families, basically lying low and waiting for an opportunity to reclaim this secret knowledge which lay under foreign jurisdiction. Some of the families involved were the Counts of Champagne, Lords of Gisors, Lords of Payen, Counts of Fontaine, Counts of Anjou, de Bouillon, St Clairs of Roslin (Rosslyn) . . . and the Habsburgs. Some families lost direct contact with each other, but the chosen sons knew the secret and how to recognise their peers. I asked myself why should this not include the House of Savoy, as they are one of the oldest established families in Europe.

## Lineage details

Tracing the lineage of the House of Savoy proved to be a minefield beyond the well-known and well-documented beginnings of the dynasty with Humbert the Whitehanded.

But then connections appeared independently which brought me back in a huge circle concerning the main protagonists already mentioned.

In the book by Laurence Gardner, the Chevalier Labhràn de St Germain *Bloodline of the Holy Grail*, the contentious bloodline from Jesus and Mary Magdalene, traced through the ages, provided me with some tantalising clues with regard to the historic lineage of the House of Savoy.

Tracing the line of descent through the Sicambrian Franks, from the union of Faramund (d. 420AD) and Princess Argotta, the major areas of interest can be found.

Firstly:

- from their son, Clodion (d.446AD), to Charles Martel (d. 741AD) – the Mayor of the Palaces of Austrasia, Neustria and **Burgundy** – through to Charlemagne (d. 814AD);
- from him, Pépin, the King of Italy (d. 810AD) and Godefroi de Bouillon (1160–1100AD), thence Baldwin I, **King of Jerusalem** (d. 1118AD.);
- equally from Charlemagne, the rulers of Eastern France, leading on to Hugh Capet (d. 996 AD.) and the Capetian dynasty.

Secondly:

- from Clodion derived eventually the **Merovingian** Line, due to be supplanted in due course by the Carolingians and Charlemagne; this line is very significant as it meets the descendants of Clodion's brother, Fredemundus, through **King Chilperic of Burgundy** (d. 504AD) whose daughter, **Clotilde of Burgundy**, became **King Clovis'** wife in 492AD;
- from this union sprang the **Merovingians**, down to Dagobert II (d. 679AD). Here we have the connections with **Rennes-le-Château** via **Razès**; also down this line are the Counts of Toulouse, such as Guilhelm de Toulouse, Master of Aquitaine, Davidic Sovereign of the Jewish state of Septimia, who died in 828AD.

To find connections here going back to Jerusalem was surprising. But then Septimania was substantially the eighth century Jewish kingdom which devolved into the region of Languedoc, the home of the **Cathars**. This area was steeped in the traditions of Lazarus and Mary Magdalene, who was regarded as the 'Grail Mother' of true Western Christianity. *They were also said to be the guardians of a great and sacred treasure, associated with a fantastic and ancient knowledge which would destroy the fundamental concept of the orthodox Roman Church.* Could the fact that this treasure has never been found or substantiated be linked with Savoy?

From **Chilperic's brother, Galains**, we eventually arrive through a myriad of connections at the Royal line of the **Stuarts,** through whom Freemasonry was promulgated in Britain. Why are they of interest? The Royal Stuart Society makes its position clear with regard to its direct and legitimate male lineage after it ended with the death, in 1807, of Henry IX, Cardinal Duke of York, the brother of Prince Charles Edward Stuart. *The line passed to the House of Savoy*, in fact to Charles Emmanuel IV of Sardinia, by virtue of its descent from Henrietta-Anne (1644–1670), daughter of King Charles I, and her husband, Philippe, Duke of Orléans. The lineage has since passed to Prince Franz of Bavaria. However, Laurence Gardner dismisses this transference as fantasy, saying that Henry IX's last will did not name Charles Emmanuel as his successor.

Whatever the truth is about this controversy, the fact remains that the House of Savoy was considered *worthy* of the lineage. The links between the early Burgundians and the later House of Savoy seem strong, as do those with the Merovingians. Other links were being suggested with the Languedoc and Rennes-le-Château along with their Cathar heritage through the Merovingians, the Counts of Toulouse and Razès.

### The direct ancestral link

It was then that the Internet provided key information, linking the House of Savoy directly to Clovis, but it was Clovis the Riparian, the Frankish king of Cologne, a 'kinsman' of Clovis the Great, but who lived a couple of generations before him. Clovis the Riparian ruled over the Upper Rhine, while Clovis ruled over the Lower (more northerly) reaches.

The connection between them is that the Riparian's grandson, Siegbert I 'the lame', was murdered by his own son, Cloderic 'the Parricide', in 509AD, at the instigation of Clovis the Great, who then promptly murdered Cloderic, to further his own claims and extend his territory. Such was the bloodthirsty and treacherous nature of the times!

The direct lineage from **Clovis, the Riparian,** to **Humbert of Savoy** is as follows. I have no reason to doubt its validity. Important connections to other dynasties are included, such as the Burgundians and the Carolingians to the Capetians:

| |
|---|
| **Clovis 'the Riparian'**: Frankish king of Cologne: living 420. |
| **Childebert**: King of Cologne: living 450. |
| **Siegbert I** 'the Lame': King of Cologne: d. 509. |
| **Cloderic** 'the Parricide': King of Cologne: d. 509. |
| **Muderic**, Lord of Vitre-en-Perthois: b.circa 500. / d. 532. |
| **St Gondolfus**, Bishop of Tongres: b. 524 AD. / d. sixth July 607. |
| **Bodegisel II**, 'Dux': b. circa 556 / d.588. |
| **St Arnulf**, Bishop of Metz / Mayor of Palace in Austrasia: b. 582 d. 640. |
| **Duke d'Angise**: Mayor of Palace in Austrasia: b. 602 / d. 685. |
| **Pépin of Heristol**: Mayor of Palace in Austrasia: b. circa 635/ d. 714. [1 son = *Charles Martel – Charlemagne – Hugh Capet of Capetian Dynasty*] |
| **Childebrand I of Autun**, Lord of Perracy & Bordgy: b. 714 / d. 751. |

| |
|---|
| **Nivelon (Nibelung) of Perracy**: Lord of Perracy, Montisan & Hesburg: d. 768. |
| **Childebrand II of Perracy**: b.(by) 768 / d. 826/836? |
| **Thierry I 'the Treasurer'**: Chamberlain to Charles the Bald: b. (by) 817/ d. (circa).880; grandson – Manases I – married *Ermengarde of Burgundy* (by Oct. 920). |
| **Richard**: living 885. |
| **Garnier (Warinus)**: Viscount of Sens & Troyes: b. circa 868 / d. 925. |
| **Hugh of Vienne**: Count Palatine of **Burgundy**: b. circa 900 / d. after 927; *married* (by 927) *Willa of Burgundy*. |
| **Humbert** (Hubert / Umberto): b. circa 926/930 / d. circa 976. |
| **Humbert I 'the Whitehanded'**: b. circa 975 / d.1048 / 1050. |

Here was my link back to Henry Lincoln's assertion that the ancestors of the Merovingians were of the holy bloodline. The House of Savoy and Clovis formed one chain, which had connections with Jerusalem.

### A Cologne connection?

It then struck me as another of those strange coincidences that Cologne should feature at the start of two 'dynasties' involved in this wide-ranging investigation.

Firstly, Clovis the Riparian was king of that city or area in the fifth century and his descendant, Humbert, began the House of Savoy dynasty. Then St Bruno was born in Cologne in the eleventh century (most probably in 1030) and ended up in the same area as Humbert's family to retire from the world. Was there a connection in the Cologne factor?

From André Ravier, I learnt that Cologne, at the time of Bruno's childhood, was the major city of Germany and had worldly importance, mainly through the efforts of its Archbishop, another Bruno, Bruno I. It was known as 'Saint Cologne' or 'German Rome'. But nothing definite remains extant about St Bruno's childhood there before he went to Reims. Of his family, they were not without some nobility. Ravier states that, in the middle of the sixteenth century, it was said that Bruno belonged to the von Hartenfaust family. But this could just be the obscure remnants of an oral tradition. The fact is that we do not know for sure.

The other intriguing thought is whether Bruno had an inkling of a powerful secret emanating from the seat of Cologne and that this coloured his subsequent route from Reims to Savoy, including a sojourn of three years in the company of St Robert of Molesmes along the way. Let us remember that Ravier states that the reason why Bruno came to Grenoble is basically unknown.

### *Rex Deus and the First Crusade*

The first Crusade provided the Rex Deus groups with a most opportune moment to reclaim their heritage – to search for the artefacts beneath the Temple while the Crusaders were once more in control of Jerusalem. As Lomas and Knight state, the Rex Deus families were at the forefront of every Crusade – a question which has perplexed historians. Once there, non Rex Deus leaders were removed and family members infiltrated the Jerusalem monarchy and the Church, to provide secure continuity of the task.

It was intriguing to realise that the Pope, Urban II, who preached for the first Crusade at the instigation of the families, was none other than the same pupil of St Bruno when he was still at Reims. It was he who summoned St Bruno to Rome some six years after he set up his settlement in the Chartreuse. It is of little wonder that the House of Savoy held the Carthusians in such esteem!

After many years of frustrated ambition, Hugues de Champagne and Hugues de Payen managed to start their excavations in 1118 under the patronage of King Baldwin II of Jerusalem and under the auspices of their new name, the Knights Hospitaller. St Bernard of Clairvaux, closely related to Hugues de Payen and whose new abbey at Clairvaux was built specially for him by Hugues de

Champagne, was set up in the new Cistercian Order. His elder brother, the Count of Fontaine, did not approve of Bernard becoming a monk, but then joined himself within a year, along with no less than 31 other family members. This smacked of a very elaborate plan. St Bernard then granted the Rule for the new group, the Knights Templar, in 1128 at the Council of Troyes, and their prominence started.

When the fall of the Templars was nigh, it is speculated that they evacuated the artefacts and treasure to Scotland and to Roslin Rosslyn, as the St Clairs were a Rex Deus family and Hugues de Payen had married into it in 1128. In fact, Lomas and Knight have found the real meaning of the term 'Ros linn' to be 'ancient knowledge passed down the generations'. According to them, the chapel is a replica of the Jerusalem Temple plan. It is a monument to Freemasonry and the impenetrable vaults are believed to conceal some artefacts of outstanding worth and importance.

So, the House of Savoy, as a Rex Deus family, could well have been a party to the Templar activities. They cultivated very good relations with the rising stars of the Church and the upsurging monastic Orders, like St Bernard and the Carthusians, so they would not really want to jeopardise any of this by revealing the 'true' nature of the Shroud to the authorities or the people, nor did they want to betray their Templar links. It seemed like a desire to keep a foot in both camps and let the truth lie dormant.

### An explanation for the Pyramid

Here then were the intrinsic links between the Cistercians, the Templars, the Shroud and the House of Savoy. Chambéry was at the centre of the geometric patterns spread around the surrounding mountains and geographical features, as if it were symbolically protected against unwelcome influences. But the question as to why the outline of the Grand Pyramid should be there at all, not to mention its obvious importance to the overall design, still posed a problem.

Lomas and Knight have found that the rituals of the

highest Masonic degrees had been suppressed by the United Grand Lodge of England about 200 years ago, with the result that Freemasonry's ultimate origins were very indistinct in the mists of time. However, their persistent research paid off and the rediscovery of them confirmed their hypothesis at every turn. The original legend pieced together from the 33° of ancient Masonic rite (and I use their description quite closely) started with a terrible flood way back in ancient history, when the secrets of the builders of civilisation were almost lost. Enoch, to preserve this knowledge for the survivors, had carved the secrets onto two great pillars which would withstand the calamity. The founders of the Egyptian civilisation (c.3200BC) are said to have found one of these pillars. Fragments of the other pillar were supposedly found later by the Jews, on the spot where Solomon's Temple was built 3000 years ago. This could have been a convenient way of not giving all the credit to the earlier Egyptians for their mysterious king-making ritual and resurrection cult.

The authors' previous book, *The Hiram Key*, had concluded that the theology of first century Jerusalem was largely derived from Egypt and that Jesus and his brother James were part of this ancient line of priests who had knowledge of their mystic and hierarchic initiations and who went on to become the Rex Deus line.

Suddenly, I had the obvious link with the Grand Pyramid via the original knowledge of the ancient Egyptians, passed on to the first century Jerusalem sect.

My imagination was beginning to stir as to what could possibly be the reason for this Pyramid linked to the House of Savoy – a probable Rex Deus family – the Carthusians, the Templars and the Cistercians of Hautecombe. A huge pentagram in the landscape, and now this affiliated pyramid. Supposing the Templars had wanted to conceal something of great value which referred back to Egypt, beyond the Temple of Solomon? Could this hamlet of Pragondran, positioned under the King's Chamber, be the French equivalent of the vaults beneath Rosslyn Chapel? The name Pragondran is formed with the word, 'Pra(z)', present-day 'prés', meaning fields or meadows, tacked onto the name of the owners, the Gondran family. This was a very ordinary explanation on the face of it.

# PART SIX: UNDER THE PYRAMID

*Vérel-Pragondran*

On consulting M.Cérino in his antiquarian bookshop in Chambéry, I was intrigued to learn more about the origin of the place-name. **Vérel** is some way below Pragondran, but on the same single road leading up from Chambéry. The name comes from Petrus Verelli, a member of the 'bourgeois'/wealthy middle-class of Chambéry in 1370.

However, the family name of **Gondran** was far more interesting. The primitive form of this name of Germanic origin is **Guntchramnus**, the name carried by a grandson of Clovis I, Guntrandus Rex. Once again, an important link was possibly being made with the history of Clovis' era.

In 561AD, Gondran took over a Burgundy starting to re-emerge in importance and with increasing influence. He could be cruel and violent, yet conciliatory and capable of profound piety. He had more character than his brothers, Chilpéric and Siegbert, who were under the influence of their rival wives, Frédégonde and Brunehaut. Savoy was then part of a kingdom which reached Auxerre, Bourges, Orléans and Sens. Perhaps the nearest battles for him were against the Lombards, a Germanic people, who invaded the plain of the Pô, henceforth called Lombardy, from 568AD, and penetrated into the valleys of the Piedmont. Violent battles took place in the high valleys and the cols were frequently crossed by plunderers in 574AD. Gondran placed troops at Suze and Aoste, constructed fortresses and assured the passes. After Gondran's death in 593AD, a power vacuum developed in the south-east except for short periods of some relative stability under Clotaire II and Dagobert; the other kings were ineffective and became known generally as the 'lazy/good-for-nothing' kings, the 'rois fainéants'.

As soon as the name of Clovis reappeared, I had the feeling that hidden links were coming to light. Could this Gondran family have been initially represented all those centuries ago by this descendant of Clovis and could there be from this link a covert reason for them acquiring this piece of poor, isolated land that nobody wanted? After all, the reference to the historical Gondran was there in the text of this guide to the origins of Savoy place-names in an antiquarian bookshop.

The difficult relief explains the isolation of this village which remained so sidelined for so long. Yet now it is the departure point of walks up into the Bauges National Park and has limited secondary home development. The parish 'Verellum a prata gontranni' is, however, ancient, existing from the start of the twelfth century and dependent on the Priory of Bassens, a suburb of Chambéry; apparently the actual name of Pragondran was added to Vérel at the end of the seventeenth century. Even at the start of the nineteenth century, this 'commune' was among the most deprived of the whole area, with rockfalls adding to the inhabitants' discomfort. Poor access accentuated its isolation up to the Second World War and in 1975 it was still the least populated parish of the area. What better recommendation could it have for concealing something of great importance all those centuries ago?

### Sonnaz

Also to be found in the books dealing with the villages of Savoy in the Chambéry Médiathèque was the information about Sonnaz, the village in the position of the Queen's Chamber.

It belonged originally to the Diocese of Grenoble, then came under the jurisdiction of the Diocese of Chambéry in 1820. Its occupation goes back a long way, to the Gallo-Roman period. However, the most interesting period is the medieval one: the de Châtillon family were accorded the château and the seigniory as vassals of Amédée VI, Count of Savoy, in 1352, and hold the same possessions today. On the religious side, Sonnaz depended on the Priory of Lémenc. The same connections seem to be resurfacing – the House of Savoy and Lémenc.

On visiting the village, I was determined to find the 'Chartreuse' mentioned on the map. It transpires that it refers to a large building in the rue de la Chartreuse. I had not realised that a strong actual connection existed here between the monks of the Chartreuse and Sonnaz apart from the 'symbolic' links I had been uncovering.

I was very kindly invited into the former dwelling of the Carthusians by the present owners, M. and Mme Bonaz, whose mother, Mme Bouvier, gave me some very interesting information. The Chartreux had had a large agricultural holding in Sonnaz, dating probably from well before the nineteenth century (noone could be sure exactly). Quite why they had chosen Sonnaz was not known by those I spoke to, nor by M. Parmentier, the former mayor, now resident in the Château, whom I later telephoned. It could quite well simply be for the flat fields spreading out east towards the immense and steep cliffs that rear up, as if shielding the higher bowl of Pragondran. These would quite likely have been fertile fields at the time.

But what really caught my attention was the tunnel that the Chartreux had excavated right behind the house, leading up the château on the hill-top behind. According to Mme Bouvier, it was to provide an emergency bolt-hole in case of danger or invasion, to escape to the safety of the château, not far above. It would have taken a great deal of time and effort to dig out, to avoid running a couple of hundred metres up the hill. She said she had ventured into it a short way, before a sense of claustrophobia and fear overcame her, but this was (just) before 1940. It had partly collapsed after the war and a grid now blocks off the entrance alongside the road [see plate 23].

A nagging feeling of possible covert operations was refusing to go away. To put it simply, why should the

**Plate 23: The tunnel built by the Carthusian monks at Sonnaz, to facilitate their quick escape from any danger. It is directly opposite the building they occupied and it leads up to the château on top of the hill. Part of it has collapsed inside.**

Chartreux be right here, in the 'Queen's Chamber', digging a tunnel? Could they have looking for something, or trying to conceal something? (There was a history of lignite being mined at Sonnaz until the 1940's, but if the Chartreux were mining it at a very early stage, why look just in a straight line directly behind their house?) My contention would be very difficult to prove, but the fact they were here at all provides another strange coincidence, and strengthened my conviction that my 'pyramid' hypothesis was not just a mere whimsy.

This apart, there is also here the curious legend about St François de Sales, whose oratory stands in the Grand Bois.

This was to commemorate the extraordinary event when his horse stumbled and his sword became detached from his side; it formed with its sheath the shape of the Cross. François, returning to Annecy from Chambéry after signing on at the Bar as a young doctor in law, saw in this sign a confirmation of his vocation. The religious theme was even taking on mythical overtones.

## Background connections

One comment of Lomas' and Knight's Rex Deus contact also had a parallel here. When the Frenchman was asked if he knew of a medieval reconstruction of Herod's Temple in Europe, he said that it was quite probable it existed (he did not know of Rosslyn) and that interest should be turned to the west wall, although he did not know why. Taking the position of Pragondran, it is beneath the extreme west summital ridge of Mt Nivolet, the south-west point of the Bauges. Was this a physical echo?

Threads of the Magdalene cult also began to reappear in my thoughts:

- the monastery of St Guilhelm le Désert at Gellone, founded by Guilhelm de Toulouse, which had been an important seat of the Magdalene cult during the ninth century, and their connections with the Burgundian line;
- St Bernard preaching the Second Crusade in 1146 at Vézelay – consecrated to Mary in 1096 – and his drafting of the Constitution for the Order of the Knights Templar in 1228, which included a requirement for 'the obedience of Bethany, the castle of Mary and Martha';
- the common interest of the Cistercians and Carthusians in Mary; the Black Madonna tradition and locations representative of Mary Magdalene going back to Queen Isis and Adam's first consort, Lilith;
- Mary, who, according to the Alexandrian doctrine, transmitted the true secret of Jesus.

The very first alignment between Myans and Mt Margeriaz

had more intriguing connections, even though they might be considered rather obscure.

The Black Madonna of Myans is representative of Isis, the female figurehead of Egyptian religion. Mary Magdalene might well have been black and originated from Egypt or Ethiopia; being an or the important apostle of Jesus and probably the one who rallied the others around her after the Crucifixion, she would have been associated with Isis as continuing the female figurehead figure. Hence she and Myans are linked, even subconsciously.

Next in alignment is the Priory of St Jeoire. This saint was revered by the Templars. The terminal and highest point in the alignment is Mt Margeriaz, whose name comes from 'Margarita' meaning 'pearl'. Margeriaz is the deformed Savoyard version over centuries of dialectic change, according to the Musée Savoisien. However, the Town Hall at les Déserts, nestling almost underneath it, gives a rather different derivation, meaning 'meadow, sheep pasture', from the latin 'malgeria, de mulgaria'.

In the recent book by Lynn Picknett, *Mary Magdalene*, there is an intriguing link with the first derivation. Through Mary, in her role as 'hierodule' or 'sacred servant', Jesus is sanctified in the biblical anointing and set apart for his sacrificial crucifixion. A distant echo of this was enacted on 16 June 1633, when Edinburgh welcomed the newly-crowned Charles I with a girl dressed as a sea-nymph. She was known as Princess Magdalene, a kind of royal princess hailing the new monarch. The sea-nymph theme echoes the ancient associations of the name 'Mary', in that her blue robe and pearl necklace were classic symbols of the sea, edged with pearly foam. Could Mt Margeriaz have been named specifically with this connection in mind, thus placing Mary Magdalene at the top of the alignment?

This mountain stands fully astride the bisecting perpendicular of the pyramid, above the King's Chamber containing Pragondran.

David Elkington, in his study entitled 'The Tomb of Isiris', in the Autumn 2003 *Journal of the Research Into Lost Knowledge Organisation*, makes a link in this direction. He states that the Pyramid itself was said to represent the pregnant womb of Isis, with the King's Chamber being the focal point of the process. Isis' name of **'Mer'** (MR) means 'beloved' and was used by the Egyptians for these monuments. Could there also be a connection here between **Mar**garita – **Mar**geriaz to Mary through Isis?

Also from Laurence Gardner, there is mentioned another intriguing tradition of the Languedoc associated with Mary, in that she is remembered as 'la Dompna del Aquae', 'the Mistress of the Waters'. She died, allegedly, in 63AD at Aix-en-Provence, whose hot springs gave it its name (aquae (waters) – acqs – Aix). To the Gnostics (and the Celts), females afforded religious veneration were often associated with lakes, wells and springs. Gnosis (knowledge) and Wisdom were connected with the female Holy Spirit which 'moved on the face of the waters' (Genesis 1:2). This was the Holy Spirit of *Sophia* held to be incarnate in Mary Magdalene. The baptismal priests of the Gospel era were described as 'Fishers'; Jesus became a 'Fisher' on being admitted to the priesthood and his dynastic line became the 'Fisher Kings'; the supposed lines of descent from Jesus and Mary preserved the maternal Spirit of Aix, becoming the 'family of the waters' – the House del Acqs; this family was prominent in Aquitaine, where Merovingian branches of the family became Counts of Toulouse and Narbonne, and Princes of the Septimanian Midi.

In Arthurian literature, the heritage of Acqs has also persisted: in Chrétien de Troyes' twelfth century *Ywain and the Lady of the Fountain*, the 'Lady' corresponds to 'la Dompna del Aquae'; Sir Thomas Mallory's *Morte d'Arthur* in 1484 adjusted the distinction phonetically from 'del Acqs' to 'du Lac', hence the notion of the 'Lady of the Lake'.

To continue the tradition, what better place than Pragondran would recall the connections than this spot directly above the largest natural lake in France – the lac du Bourget – and the adjoining spa town of **Aix**-les-Bains?

# PART SEVEN: TEMPLAR LINKS WITH THE SAVOY REGION

## Béatrice of Savoy

The most obvious link that was brought to my attention was that created by Béatrice of Savoy, the second child of Count Thomas I and Béatrice-Marguerite of Geneva.

She married Raymond Bérenger V, Count of Provence, in December 1220, who was said to be the most powerful prince of Italy of the time. By marrying Béatrice, his court had become the centre of letters, of gallantry and courtliness. Troubadours and poets flocked there in search of patronage.

According to Guichenon, in his *Histoire de la Royale Maison de Savoie*, Béatrice was unique in the fact that she had four daughters, of whom three were Queens and one Empress, and three grand-daughters, of whom two were Queens and the other Empress. The details are as follows:

Her elder daughter, Marguerite de Provence, married 'Saint' Louis, king of France, in 1234. Léonore de Provence married Henry III, King of England, in 1236. Sancie de Provence was married to Richard of England, Count of Cornwall and Poitou, in 1243, and he became Emperor. Her other daughter Béatrice de Provence, in 1255, married Charles of France, King of Sicily and Jerusalem, and who was also the brother of 'Saint' Louis. As for her grand-daughters, Isabelle of France was Queen of Navarre, Marguerite of England became Queen of Scotland, and Béatrice of France and Sicily became Empress of Constantinople.

This dynastic success story is unprecedented, and a former link in the chain with the Carthusians reappears:

'Saint' Louis and his gift to them of a Black Virgin statuette. The power and prestige wielded by Béatrice at the time must have been enormous. Her husband also gave her lands and some castles, among which a certain Châteauneuf appears – this dated from 1238. The theme of certain connections comes back into the reckoning!

But immediately after the death of her husband, her fourth son-in-law, Charles of Anjou, tried to make inroads into her estate. The problematic settlement was presided over by 'Saint' Louis, and, broken-hearted through her enforced losses, she withdrew to the château of les Echelles, where she founded, in 1260, the Commandery of St John of Jerusalem. Les Echelles lies immediately beyond the north-west sector of the Chartreuse, on the boundary between Savoy and Isère, about 10 km south-west of Chambéry.

This Order of Knights Hospitaller was founded in Palestine in 1048 and was set up in 1309 on the island of Rhodes. The highest level of hierarchy dealing with les Echelles was the Grand Prieuré of Auvergne, amongst whose 56 commanderies was counted this one. Their main work consisted of helping travellers along isolated and usually dangerous roads, distributing alms for the poor and generally doing good works. Their organisation was distinct from the Templars, mainly through this major principle, although some aims can be seen to be synonymous, especially that of establishing a military capability. There were links with the Chartreux over land grants and the founding charter was overseen by the Archbishop of Vienne and Jean de Lion Lambert, the Abbot of Hautecombe. So links with the main 'players' were still prominent, although they were at a later date.

Béatrice died in 1266, and was buried in a splendid mausoleum; but her remains were brutally removed by revolutionaries and thrown on the tip. However, her skull was retrieved and was eventually transported to Hautecombe, to be buried in the tomb of Boniface, her brother, Archbishop of Canterbury. The incomparable treasure which was a legacy of Béatrice was moved from les

Echelles to the Château of Chambéry in the Sainte Chapelle, from where it was transferred to the convent of St Dominic. Yet again it was plundered by revolutionaries and its whereabouts are unknown.

Although this link with another Templar institution is interesting in its clear relationship with the House of Savoy and its proximity to Chambéry, I did not consider it of great importance to the main line of my investigation at first.

Then I came across a few telling lines in Piers Paul Read's *The Templars*. Although officially both Orders were trying to remain neutral throughout the crusade against the Cathars, Read states that the Hospitallers were faithful to Raymond VI and Pedro II, whereas the Templars sided with the Crusaders when both were drawn into the conflict. If we accept, nonetheless, on the contrary, as many authors have done, that the Templars did try to help the Cathars, then Read establishes a good link between the latter and the Hospitallers as well. This is shown by the fact that, when King Pedro II of Aragon died at the Battle of Muret, the Hospitallers were granted permission to retrieve his body from the battlefield. In similar vein, when Raymond VI died in 1222, they were given charge of his body and tried unsuccessfully to get permission from a number of popes to have the body interred in hallowed ground.

So, sympathies of both Orders were weighted towards the Cathars. Béatrice founded the commandery at les Echelles when she would have felt mightily aggrieved against the French monarchy and her relatives through her enforced loss of titles and possessions. King Louis was instrumental in bringing the Cathars' religious reign to an end in the Languedoc. Could she have played a part in the germ of an idea which was forming in my imagination and which involved the treasure of the Cathars?

Appearing to be of much importance in this respect is another Templar commandery in the Drôme – Richerenches.

## *Richerenches and a vital donation*

Also in Read's book is a map showing the major Templar preceptories and castles in the west in the mid-twelfth century. The nearest one to Savoy is Richerenches, in the Drôme, to the north of Provence and alongside the Rhône Valley, between Montélimar and Roaix.

Just when I was trying to find more information in the Grenoble Archives about Richerenches, but without much success, I stumbled upon a new magazine, *Templarium*.

In the edition I found, no.4, there was Richerenches as the main title of the contents! This was a very happy coincidence, as it established a very important connection with the Carthusians, on page 10 of the magazine, to be precise.

Its spiritual affiliations were initially with the Abbey of Notre-Dame d'Aiguebelle, then with the Chartreux . . . but of the **Val St Hugon**! This was the very same north-east point of my huge 32 km long diagonal which led to the pentagram and then the pyramid around Chambéry. It also answered more fully my previous discovery in the Grenoble archives that Templars had helped with the founding of St Hugon.

The Carthusians asked the Templars of Richerenches to grant them their possessions in the valley so as to unite them with their own. This was done during 1173 and 1174. The Templars stipulated they wanted, in return, to participate in the spiritual benefits of the Order of the Carthusians. So the latter founded this monastery on former Templar land and possessions. This was a surprise to learn that Templar influence extended so far north from their seat in the Drôme, but it tied in definitively both Orders to the founding of St Hugon and therefore to the geometry in the landscape. But did the Templars know about the precise location chosen by the Carthusians? Was it an unwitting transference of land? Let us note that it was at the request of the Chartreux that the land was granted.

# PART EIGHT: A LOGICAL HYPOTHESIS

## *The links to the Cathar Treasure*

Some time before my interest in the geography, history and geometry of the area around Chambéry became all-consuming, I had been very interested in the Cathar legacy, partly as a result of Henry Lincoln's forays into its historical ramifications and partly from a possible personal historical link, made known to me by an external source. The château of Usson was mentioned to me as a place of personal importance. Intrigued by this unexpected information, I accordingly visited Montségur and Usson, among other destinations, although the latter was ostensibly under some renovation. It was a striking place to visit, on the river frontier between the Aude and the Ariège, and high up on a promontory.

On visiting the region, I marvelled at the vertiginous strongholds and generally found it fascinating as to its unanswered questions. But I did not connect this area and its history to what my early research then led me in the Chartreuse. The time span was offset and the distance between the two areas would seem to preclude any real connections.

It was after giving a lecture to the Saunière Society at Newbattle Abbey near Edinburgh that a more detailed private exposé of my findings to two American colleagues gave them food for thought. They did not specify what was on their minds, but agreed with me that something of great import could only warrant the monumental effort involved in creating the landscape geometry. At the time, I had not yet fully made the local connections with the Cistercians, nor the House of Savoy, nor found the pyramid geometry. I have, as detailed above, subsequently discovered an ever-widening web of historical connections, but without finding the proof positive of what the strands were pointing towards. Then the Cathars were mentioned in a different context and I began to ponder. My thoughts were turning around Mary Magdalene at the time and I began wondering if there could, after all, be a link. After all, there are two Black Madonnas in the parish church of the village of Montségur, as Lynn Picknett states in her *Mary Magdalene*.

The Knights Templar were accused of worshipping a bearded head. She quotes an old Templar saying that 'He who owns the head of John the Baptist rules the world'. This rather odd and grisly relic has been the focal point of many books. Could it have been appropriated by Jesus from Herod's palace and used for its mystical, supernatural or 'magical' powers? It must be remembered that this era was one of Egyptian 'magical' practices. This relic would have bestowed great power and glory on its owner. The Talmud indicates that Jesus himself was trained in Egyptian magic. This prized possession would have become a holy Grail and the Grail was traditionally kept and protected by women. The heretical Christian underground movement believed that Mary Magdalene finished up by being the custodian of the head, or guardian of the Grail. The inner circle of the Templars was also the reputed custodians of the Grail. Jean Markale, a specialist in Celtic studies at the Sorbonne [see select bibiography], writes that in the thirteenth century, certain German intellectual groups were convinced that a link existed between the Cathar heretics and the Grail guardians, thereby implying that the Grail could be a Cathar talisman. The Grail cycle, although belonging to the Arthurian group, emphasises a secret royal lineage, a dynasty traced back to King David. The references seemed to be going in circles.

Picknett postulates the theory that if Mary brought it to France, could it have been the 'treasure', or part of it, that the Cathars spirited away from Montségur? She states that the Inquisition had no doubt that they believed it had fallen into the hands of the Cathars. It was probably one part of the treasure, the other being their own version of the gospels. One corroboratory point is that churches dedicated to the Baptist in the Languedoc and southern France tend to be close to those dedicated to the Magdalene, as if, as Picknett says, they were spiritually inseparable.

Another intriguing bit of 'evidence' is in Saunière's altar-piece in the church at Rennes-le-Château, where Mary is depicted kneeling before a skull and an open book, possibly representing the Baptist's head and the lost gospel(s).

I went back to revise quickly Henry Lincoln's conclusions in the *Holy Blood and the Holy Grail*, beginning with the Parfaits' escape from Montségur with some kind of documentary(?) evidence, deemed too deadly to the Church to tolerate and of great importance to the Cathars; then the link with Saunière's quest, his obsession with Mary Magdalene and his sudden vast financial resources; the geometry in the landscape and elsewhere; and the all-important line of descent from Jesus and Mary Magdalene, through the Merovingians, as reported by the shadowy Prieuré of Sion. Again, could this 'treasure' be, in fact, a gospel written by Mary Magdalene and discovered by the Cathars – a gospel containing the true teaching of Christ rejected by the Pauline Church?

Many books have sought to explain the precise nature of it and where it might have gone. The mere hint of the Holy Grail unleashes a plethora of potential solutions and explanations. A myriad of researchers have scoured the Cathar area and are still doing so.

Then *L'Hérésie Cathare* furnished more cogent inform-ation. Three declarations were made to the Inquisition by men-at-arms defending Montségur. They were made freely and the soldiers – Arnaud Roger de Mirepoix, Bérenger de Lavelanet and Guilhem de Bouan – were then left at liberty by the Catholic Church, so there is no reason to suppose torture was used to extract the information. There was also the declaration of Bernard de Joucou. They heard of the escape with the 'treasure' from the besieged castle without witnessing it themselves, it has to be admitted, but they name three of the four involved: Amiel Ricard (Aicart?), Augé, and Poitevin (Peytavi?). The leader of the Cathar garrison, Pierre-Roger de Mirepoix, helped them. They escaped by night by means of ropes down the cliff face, so the 'treasure' could not have been heavy quantities of money, gold or silver; instead, it is alleged that it consisted of crucial documents whose spiritual importance warranted them being kept at Montségur until this late date.

According to Markale, the negotiations between the Inquisition and the Montségur defenders, Pierre-Roger de Mirepoix and Ramon de Perella, were conducted under the safeguard of Ramon d'Aniort, lord of Rennes-le-Château and Rennes-les-Bains. A fire was lit on the summit of Bidorta by Escot de Belcaire, Ramon's special envoy, to alert the besieged defenders of Montségur that the escape operation had been a success. Ramon d'Aniort, despite being a rebel and heretic whose possessions were at first seized and who was excommunicated, was then received and indulged by Louis IX. Was this a result of Ramon's knowledge of a 'treasure', indicating documents proving the existence and survival of a Merovingian line, the legitimate dynasty usurped by the Carolingians and Capets? This might explain 'Saint' Louis'[see Addendum 2] ambiguous attitude towards certain Cathar leaders and allies as well as leading us onto Bérenger Saunière of Rennes-le-Château.

Indeed, the links go further. Louis IX's mother, Blanche de Castille, persuaded her son to pardon Raymond VII, Count of Toulouse, after his rebellion following the massacre of the Inquisitors at Avignonnet. It was perhaps her primary influence and fears of this hidden 'treasure' kept by the Cathars that explain her ambivalent attitude and link her throughout historical folklore to the Razès, and the area around Rennes-le-Château.

When it is realised that Louis' mother-in-law was Béatrice de Savoie, who might well have been a conduit, unwitting or otherwise, in the smuggling away of this 'treasure' to her homeland of Savoy through her contacts as wife of Raymond Bérenger V, Count of Provence, the reasons for her downfall might just be more secretive, or even vengeful, than hitherto accepted.

The other unheralded evidence which provides a vital link with my hypothesis is provided by the research of Charles Montésault in 1769. He was one of only two people to bring to light a text in old French deposited with a solicitor in the region. This text was highlighted again in 1937 by Romain Gassan. The text states that one of those to escape from Montségur was a *Templar* who led the fugitives to a group of men *who escorted them to a secure place of refuge.* A flight of fancy? Apparently, Montésault gave the name of the Templar which is corroborated in other documents.

He also documents other operations by the Templars to help the Cathars, which would seem to be at odds with some authors, for example Read. Several properties were very rapidly acquired, but not run, by the Templars, at sites near strongholds favourable to Catharism and each time bought quickly during periods of conflict. Profit can be ruled out as a motive, as these properties were never exploited for their turnover. Markale highlights the conclusion that there was an active complicity between the Cathars and the Templars and adds the suggestion that the latter were the formers' secular arm, as the Cathars were prohibited from bearing arms. Indeed, he is of the opinion that the Templars were very often the protectors of the Cathars, thereby going against the most elementary rules of the Catholic Church.

The more I delved, the closer the escape was linked to the Templar movement.

The basic story of the escape is wellknown, but I began to wonder if the research has been done in the wrong place. If the 'treasure', assuming of course that it exists, was so important, would it have been wise to keep it in the same area? Would it not have been better served by moving it to a far-flung secure location? Could the area of my research possibly fit the bill?

Then the various religious and historical links I had discovered began to cross-reference with the threads from Lincoln's research. Savoy was next to France but safe from its immediate incursions. But could the geographical gap be breached?

I searched for more information on the Internet about Usson. Three French sites chosen at random state quite categorically that the Parfaits who escaped with the 'treasure' passed through Usson, as there were very close links between it and Montségur. But then the trail of the Cathar 'treasure' goes cold. Where could they have been going? Most would assume that a good hiding place in the Pyrenees would have sufficed. However, that route leads equally well towards Pradès and the coast at Perpignan over a pass and down main valleys.

At this juncture, by chance, a lawyer colleague, John McCann, lent me a book on the subject by Jonathan Sumption, *The Albigensian Crusade*, and vital clues were forthcoming. Although he states that, referring to the Parfaits' escape, 'Of the nature of the hoard and the success of their venture, nothing more is known beyond the fruitless speculations of romantic imaginings', a few sections of his book enabled me to make considerable strides.

He states that, after Montségur, the minority clinging to their faith did so in the most clandestine, and usually natural, surroundings. Some fled to Catalonia, where the Inquisition was intermittent, or to Italy, where it was ineffective. He cites Pierre Bauville, a conspirator of Avignonet, who fled to Lombardy in 1245, and found colonies of exiled Cathars wherever he went. He mentions other locations, such as Coni, Piacenza and Cremona. These remnants of the Cathar faith were able to exist for a while in Italy and they were able to make their way there.

Markale does state that the besieged Cathars in Montségur were able to evacuate their treasure through the efforts of four 'Parfaits'. Other survivors, dedicated to the salvation and maintenance of Catharism, also escaped from other previous havens. The quest for some refuge depended partly on the previous existence of seven Cathar bishoprics – or rather 'territories' – in Italy at the highpoint of the heresy's development, between 1150 and 1240. The other strongholds in France had been Champagne, plus Albi, Toulouse, Carcassonne, Comminges, Razès and Agen – in other words, the domains of the count of Toulouse. After

1244, the organisation collapsed and Catharism re-grouped in the upper Ariège valley around Tarascon. He confirms also that many, however, fled to Lombardy.

Did they sail to Italy or take a land route? It was when I compared two maps in Sumption's book that possibilities suddenly emerged, if a land route was taken, or one by sea to Provence, presumably from the area of Perpignan.

Putting together the maps showing, firstly, Languedoc in 1204 – territorial divisions of loyalty, and, secondly, Languedoc and the major places involved in the time of the crusade, made the area loyalties clear [see figure 17]. I had not realised that Provence and the Rhône valley right up to the north of Valence (the County and Marquisate of Provence) were loyal to Raymond VI.

In the Provence of the time of the fall of Montségur, Béatrice de Savoie would have been at or near the height of her power. Her father, Count Thomas I, had made Chambéry his capital in 1232. Her influence spread all the way back up the Rhône valley and adjoining areas to the north of Provence right to Chambéry. Large Templar preceptories had been set up in the previous century right through this area, namely St Gilles, Arles, Avignon, Roaix and **Richerenches**, before arriving at Veurey-Voroize, to the immediate north-west of Grenoble, so there must have been some mingling of interests between the extensive Templar influence and the Court of Raymond and Béatrice.

As the Templars and the Hospitallers were sympathetic to the Cathars, and Provence was loyal to Raymond VI, this could have provided a network to spirit away any refugees from danger, including any precious cargo they had with them. Italy was a destination for some, but Savoy would have been very accessible. Richerenches was the closest main Templar preceptory to Savoy of great importance; then came Béatrice's founding of the Hospitaller centre of les Echelles. We must not forget the important link between Richerenches and the Carthusians with regard to the granting of the land for St Hugon some 70 years earlier.

What had initially seemed very obtuse as an idea now seemed far more feasible. The sacred geometrical imagery

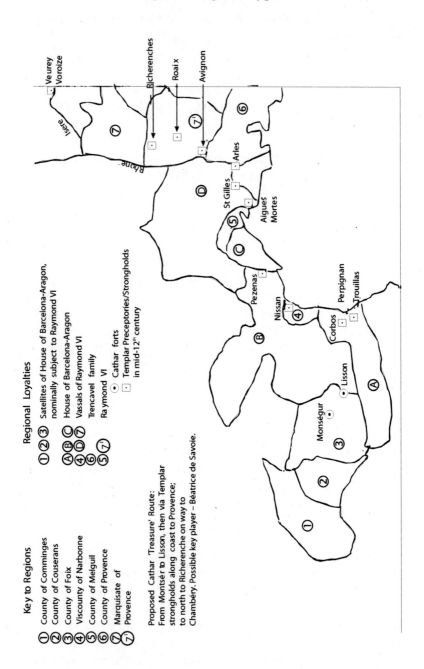

Key to Regions

① County of Comminges
② County of Couserans
③ County of Foix
④ Viscounty of Narbonne
⑤ County of Melguil
⑥ County of Provence
⑦ Marquisate of Provence

Regional Loyalties

①②③ Satellites of House of Barcelona-Aragon, nominally subject to Raymond VI
Ⓐ Ⓑ Ⓒ House of Barcelona-Aragon
④ Ⓓ ⑦ Vassals of Raymond VI
⑥ Trencavel family
⑤ ⑦' Raymond VI

◉ Cathar forts
▫ Templar Preceptories/Strongholds in mid-12ᵗʰ century

Proposed Cathar 'Treasure' Route:
From Montsé to Lisson, then via Templar strongholds along coast to Provence; to north to Richerenche on way to Chambéry. Possible key player – Béatrice de Savoie.

134

in the landscape, the long historically important lineage of the House of Savoy, their collusion with the early Orders of monks and the Templars, all provide a possible answer to this ancient mystery. Markale states towards the start of his book that the pentagram was a commonly used symbol of the Cathars, but that its exact meaning for them still remains mysterious. It is more the route to and location of the possible hiding-place, rather than being able to state what exactly is (or was?) there that is apparent. Markale, however, considers the problem is not so much learning the location of the 'treasure' as discovering what it was! For I find it hard to believe that the purpose of such monumental feats of surveying and such careful co-ordinated planning by different groups of people over so long could have been forgotten or lost. Whatever is, or even perhaps was, located at Pragondran must be of immense importance to have warranted such a huge investment of effort to create the geometry pointing towards it. My supposition is that it may be the Cathar Treasure, or some startling new evidence involving Mary Magdalene.

As an exercise in logic and to try to clarify the main sequential threads of influence over the historical background, I tried linking them on one sheet. The result might aid comprehension [see figure 28], although there was more to add later.

## Names

While trying to wade through the allegorical background to the legends of King Arthur and the links to the Holy Grail, I found that 'Pendragon' basically means 'the great leader'. Just as Saint Graal (Holy Grail) can be interpreted as 'Sang

---

**Figure 17 (facing page): A plan of the proposed route of the Cathar 'treasure' from Montségur, via Usson Castle, to the Templar preceptory of Richerenches, thence to Savoy. The background of areas loyal to the Cathar cause and major Templar centres would have facilitated its transfer.**

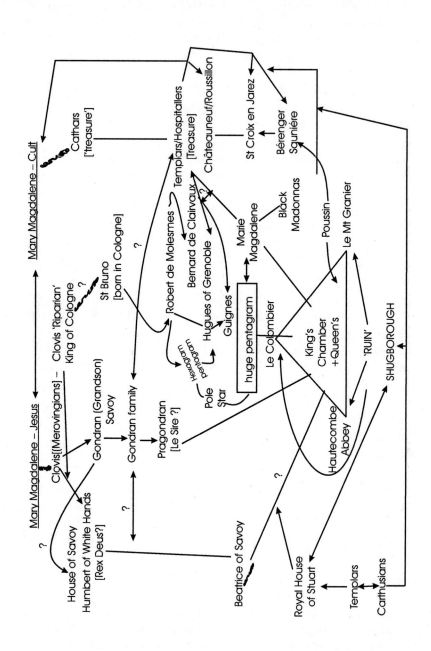

Royal' or 'Royal Blood(line)', it struck me that Vérel-Pragondran could become 'Vrai Réel Pendragon' or 'True Real Great Leader'! Just a play on words?

However, what struck me as of possibly greater significance, is the name of the first slope/high point of the cliff ridge immediately behind Pragondran in the furthest north-east corner of the cliff bowl. If this really is the equivalent/replica of the King's Chamber in the Great Pyramid, it is an amazing coincidence that this part of the ridge is called **'le Sire'** or **'Sire'**, **'Lord'**, **'Saviour'**. My efforts to try to discover the origin of this name sent me on a lengthy chase from one place of reference to another, until finally Mme Laurence Sadoux-Troncy of the Musée Savoisien in Chambéry sent me an explanation which was not what I was hoping for, but which made sense.

The names 'Sir, Sira, Seille' refer to *'the wind which brings snow'* and is used in the Alps and the southern Massif Central. In his *Trésor du Félibrige*, (a Provençal reference work), the author, Mistral, usually gives the origin of the words he describes, be they romanesque, Celtic, Germanic, Arabic or Hebrew, but for 'Cira' he gives nothing. According to the pronunciation, however, there could well be a Turkish root. An eastern European/Asian link was intriguing, considering where my research into Cathar origins had led me, namely the Bogomils and the Balkans.

Could this name have a double meaning? If so, then my assertion of the 'King's Chamber' overlaying this site would certainly gain weight.

On trying to get more local information about the origins of le Sire, I contacted the secretariat of the mayor's office in

-----

**Figure 28 (facing page): a schematic plan of the lines of research and their interplay of influence, both horizontally and vertically, which suggested itself towards the end of this part of my research. Some connections are necessarily speculative, especially that between Jesus and Mary Magdalene at the start, but the major figures of influence are included.**

Vérel-Pragondran and spoke at some length to Mme Etallaz. She had spent most of her working life there but did not know the dialectic meaning of the title. So at least I could provide some information! While on holiday at Challes-les-Eaux, I saw her at the Town Hall in Vérel; she dug out the oldest maps of the parish they possessed dating from about 1864, along with earlier acts of marriages and births from 1828. The evidence for the name was there, but I could go no further back than these dates, unfortunately.

However, other items of information surfaced which were most illuminating.

She said that the Chartreux had been interested in buying land at Pragondran over a long period of time, but no one wanted to sell land to them. Specifically, they had wanted to establish a chapel at about 1800/1820. This was certainly glad tidings for my investigations, as it had been for Sonnaz. Why would they want to get a footing in this remote spot, unless the remoteness was the main reason in itself? Yet there was a hamlet already nearby, which seemed to defeat the object.

Her other snippet of information led me into an area of research I had not envisaged doing until then. According to her grandmother, there was a legend about a subterranean lake under Mt Nivolet, which immediately created a link to the limestone caves already discovered at le Doria and under Mt Margeriaz which are on the other side of the mountain. Could the fissures apparent in the rockface on this side of the massif above Pragondran lead to hitherto undiscovered caves behind? Difficult access and rockfalls over the centuries have made this prospect unappealing. Mme Etallaz confirmed that no known archeological research has ever been properly undertaken here.

One other odd name that is extant on old and modern maps is the 'gorges de Bac(c)hus', just alongside the singular feature described in the next section. Mme Etallaz found both spelling variations on her old maps and confirmed that it was not a family name. Could this be an oblique reference to another 'god' figure, or was it more prosaic? Mme Sadoux-Troncy of the Savoy Museum said of Bachus that the word was a dialectic corruption of 'bachal, bachat, bachau, bachet, bachu, bassu...etc', meaning 'a large basin/receptacle made from wood or stone'. I can see the resemblance with the outline of the little semi-circular gorge, but even so . . . !

Two overt spellings of lordly and pagan mythogical figures in this small remote spot?

In an effort to get further with le Sire's origins, I went to the Town Hall at les Déserts in whose commune le Sire actually lies. This village is at the entrance to the plateau below la Féclaz, a ski resort behind Mt Nivolet. I was again made to feel most welcome by Monique, the secretary, and by the mayor, Gérard Dumaz. They were both unaware of the 'wind which brings snow' origin of le Sire, and also produced a map of the relevant part of the commune dating from 1865 which was the earliest documentary proof of the site. By an odd quirk of fate, Monique said her relatives were among the earliest known inhabitants of this spot. To be precise, it was the great-grandfather of M.André Radici, who is her uncle, I believe. In those times, many people in the locality had the same names, so to distinguish between them, they took the place name as an addition to their own. I was also given a photo of the great-grandfather as a youngster posing with his family in front of the chalet in the early 1900s. The approximate date and family connections were confirmed by another local inhabitant, a joiner, M. Vuillerme, who could give me no other meaning of le Sire apart from what I knew already.

### The Precise Spot?

From a vantage point, I had scoured the cliff walls above Pragondran especially on the side of le Sire, trying to imagine where the best possible place to conceal something of immense value would be. Obviously, perhaps, in a cave, rather than buried underground, but there did not seem to be any outstanding one, at least visible from the village. I tried approaching them from below, but, at this first attempt, the wooded slopes were almost impossible to get up and the view upwards was totally obscured by the trees.

## Part Eight: A Logical Hypothesis

I went across to the other side of the 'bowl' to take a photo of Sonnaz way below the cliff edge, across the valley below. On returning, I stopped in my tracks, as I then noticed for the first time, in the cliff at the other right-hand end of the face towards Mt Nivolet, next to the 'gorges de Bacchus', what appeared to be a cave/crevice in the form of a cross. I had the impression that one part of the cross-section seemed chiselled – to accentuate the shape? Was it a trick of the light? It was difficult to see clearly, even with binoculars, but it would certainly be a fitting end to my investigation to find the location of the 'treasure' in a cave marked by the Christian symbol! Could this feature really be the entrance to a cave, both inaccessible and big enough to serve as a depository, or, if not the actual precise spot, could it be a sign that this hamlet really was the end of the trail, that this natural symbol, by figuratively hanging beside it, marked a 'sacred' site?

The problem of reaching it reminded me of the (supposed?) manner of the escape from Montségur with ropes being used to lower the men down the cliff-face at night. In contrast, this would appear to be much simpler, even though the steeply sloping wooded area immediately above this cliff section would make a secure anchoring point the main worry. I had walked the horizontal path above these cliffs and that leading from Pragondran up towards Mt Nivolet, which passes to the side of them, on a number of occasions, but I had never noticed this feature before.

The thought did occur to me that, if the Cathars rejected the idea of the cross, it would be ironic if their sacred documents were hidden behind, or in the shadow of, the very same symbol. But the Templars would surely have been instrumental in establishing the site with its geometry, so the cross-like shape would serve as a very visible indicator or signpost overlooking the whole bowl of Pragondran.

The next stage was to investigate the cross at close quarters.

Very recently I tried to get as close as possible to the base of the cliff underneath the cross. This was no easy task, fighting my way up over scree and loose earth covered with leaves and twigs under a fairly dense tree panoply. Certainly the difficulty reaching the wall was a trump card for anyone looking for inaccessibility. Climbing up would be a daunting task, but I did not have enough time to scour along the bottom of the cliff to see if any part was easier to access.

The one partial success was to obtain the closest photo I could of the cross, when the panoply parted sufficiently on my way up. A few seconds later, the heavens opened with the onset of a large storm.

### The speleology of the cardinal areas.

When Mme Etallaz had mentioned her grandmother's comments about a lake underneath Mt Nivolet, I wondered about the possibility of cave systems within this extreme western side of the massif. The underground water system leading to the Doria cave and waterfall between Mt Nivolet and Mt Peney was an obvious pointer, but it was a fair distance from Pragondran.

Looking further into the possibilities at the Médiathèque, I was astonished to realise that there are three main areas of cave systems around Chambéry and that they correspond to the major points of my investigations: namely, the Féclaz plateau, the Margeriaz massif and the Granier massif.

Under the La Féclaz plateau, the longest network of connected galleries is about 21 km long. This network runs north-south from the 'Creux de la Cavale' and the 'Creux des Psylos' to the north and the 'Trou du Garde' to the north-west of la Féclaz, joining the system of the 'Creux de Pleurachat' south of la Féclaz which gushes forth into the Doria waterfall [see figures 18 and 19].

With regard to corresponding latitudes, but positioned apart over a small distance, le Sire is situated just to the north of the Creux de Pleurachat while the gorges de Bacchus are about half-way between it and the Grotte de la Doria. It would seem a very logical assumption that there could well be as yet undiscovered gallery systems which would link up the very cliffs I was studying above Pragondran to the extensively, but not exhaustively,

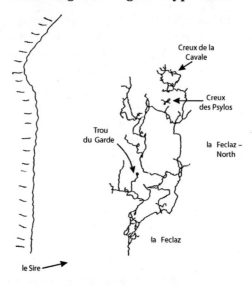

**Figure 18: A basic outline of the major underground water systems beneath the Féclaz plateau. Le Sire is just to the south-west of this part of the network.**

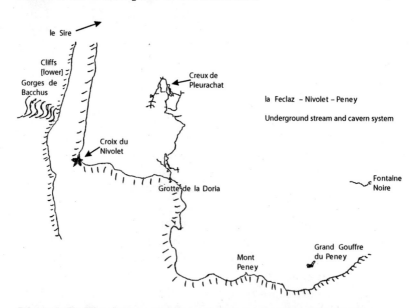

**Figure 19: The lower section of the same area, where the cliffs above Pragondran are a short distance from the 'Creux de Pleurachat'.**

142

searched network of caves and potholes further to the east The distance involved is roughly only one kilometre. What I had imagined were just a few possible isolated and relatively inaccessible cave entrances could now become part of a much bigger picture of underground systems. Surely the creators of a sophisticated geometrical pattern in the landscape would have been aware to some extent of these underground systems, even up to a thousand years ago?

Mt Margeriaz is a famous training-ground for cavers as it boasts an extensive system, linked by potholes known as

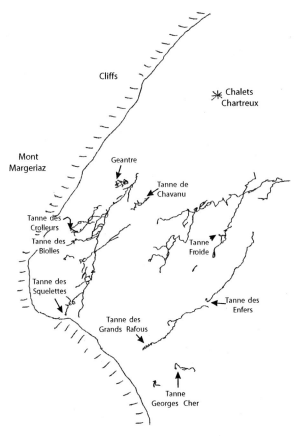

**Figure 20: The 'tannes' and associated systems of Mt Margeriaz. The Chalets Chartreux ruins are marked for reference.**

**Plate 24: The Chalets Chartreux on Mt Margeriaz. This stone marks the entrance to the site, although it is not at all obvious in the undergrowth.**

**Plate 25: The Chalets Chartreux. The typical remains of the ruins – just the remnants of the walls.**

'tannes'. The most intricate section is directly below the summit, featuring three tannes, '-des Squelettes',-des Biolles' and '-des Crolleurs'; then long galleries snake their way north-eastwards down the back of the mountain [see figure 20]. It should be remembered that Mt Margeriaz is pivotal to the major first alignment in the Chambéry valley as well as being central to the pyramid.

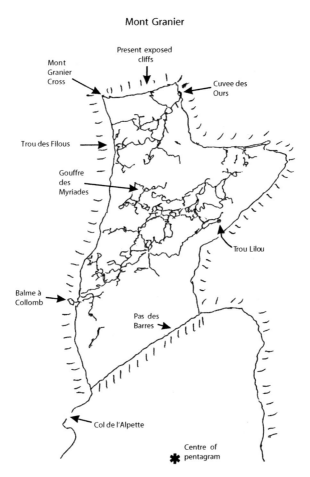

Mont Granier

Figure 21: The underground watercourses of Mt Granier to the north of the centre of the pentagram. There are also innumerable potholes littering the whole area.

# Part Eight: A Logical Hypothesis

I was most interested to note that the Chartreux had been active in this area as well. The ruins of their 'chalets' lie to the immediate north-east of the main pothole system. Nothing much remains of their settlement which is very overgrown [see plates 24 and 25]. Smelting or forestry would seem to have been their main preoccupations, but traces of them always appear in the salient places.

Mt Granier, the most obvious landmark forming the primordial link between the Chartreuse, the Chambéry valley and the Bauges, is riddled with potholes and underground systems.Those mapped fall into the northern section, just beyond the centre-point of the huge pentagram [see figure 21]. Yet Mt Pinet to the immediate south-west is infamous for its dangerous terrain, especially in winter when the numerous crevasses and potholes are hidden by treacherous snow.

Is it purely by chance that these limestone formations are right underneath some of the most important places involved in my research? I was not aware of their extent until right at the end, which I feel lends weight to my conclusions.

# SECTION THREE

# PART ONE: THE SHUGBOROUGH CONNECTION

### *An unexpected solution to the Shepherd's Monument enigma*

Shugborough has been a National Trust House since 1966, lived in by Lord Lichfield, in Staffordshire. It was the principal seat of the Anson family since the seventeenth century and was a place of pilgrimage for art connoisseurs and those appreciative of nature in harness. Thomas Anson inherited it in 1720 and welcomed his cultivated and well-travelled friends to it, including James 'Athenian' Stuart, an architect renowned for his neo-Classical monuments. Thomas Anson's younger brother, George, provided the fortune that allowed freer rein to the improvements to the estate. George became Admiral of the Fleet, and is recognised as the 'father' of the British Navy. It is next to Cannock Chase and has 18 acres of gardens, and 900 acres of parkland, woodland and farmland. A number of ley-lines cross the estate, according to my 'guide', Russell Gethings.

It also has historic monuments, of which the two most 'perplexing' (the guidebook's own words) are: the Ruin and the Shepherd's Monument.

The Ruin stands by the landing stage at the river end of the terraced garden. It was once far more extensive and embraced a gothic dovecote. Seated on the rubble crag are the remains of a druid made from coadestone. It was at least in part the work of Thomas Wright. Three puzzling elements of this aroused my immediate interest and to which I shall return.

The Shepherd's Monument [see plate 27] is the more

149

**Plate 27: The Shepherd's Monument. The mirror image of Poussin's original painting is clear, although the vagaries of the weather have left their mark. The enigmatic inscription is evident, but the 'D' and 'M' at the bottom need delineating for clarity.**

enigmatic. It was probably built c.1750 and was designed again by Thomas Wright, completed by James Stuart. The monument takes its name from the marble relief (in mirror image), based on the painting by Nicholas Poussin, *Et in Arcadio Ego* or *les Bergers d'Arcadie* (1640–2). This depicts a scene in Arcadia, a mythical paradise, where two lovers in pastoral dress listen attentively to a shepherd, pointing out to them the above engraved 'Et in Arcadia Ego' on a large tomb, with a distinctive mountainous backdrop on the horizon. On a tablet below the relief is a cryptic inscription:

O.U.O.S.V.A.V.V.

D.                                    M.

This has remained an enigma for two and a half centuries, despite many asserted solutions and countless attempts to solve it.

When this enigma was aired in the national press during the autumn of 2004, it was emphasised for how long no comprehensive solution had been found for it and how the professional code-breakers of Bletchley Park had been commandeered to apply their expertise. The relatively few letters involved certainly make it very difficult to break. Indeed, one code-breaker stated that unless you had an idea of the other end solution to work towards, it was almost impossible, as the sequence is too short to establish a workable pattern.

I too had read the press with interest without having a clear idea of any way of progressing and not even putting more than a cursory thought to it. If experts are stumped, then what hope is there for us mere mortals? Then a few days later, late at night after re-reading some notes on the Chartreuse, I realised that a nagging memory of something vaguely reminiscent was trying to force its way into my mind. Infuriatingly, it took a few days to crystallise exactly what.

The answer was a picture of the *Carthusian emblem* on the front of a magazine I had bought some ten tears ago: a cross surmounting a globe with the motto '**Stat Crux Dum Volvitur Orbis**' ('The Cross remains while the world turns') in a semi-circle around the lower half of the globe (see figure 22). The double 'O's and all the 'V's stuck out in my mind.

Relieved at having identified the connection, I was still left to equate the two, as a straight comparison between the initial letters patently did not work – this would have been far too easy! However, there are echoes which made me begin to consider the problem laterally. I deliberately took into account that the Carthusian emblem is pictorial, like the Poussin painting (obviously); but the latter is also based on *pentagonal* geometry, as Henry Lincoln showed from Professor Cornford's study of it. If I could see this inscription as a diagram, then perhaps it would make sense.

The 'O's, 'V's, 'S', 'D' and 'M' could all be found in the emblem, but what was the pattern?

**Figure 22: The Carthusian emblem of 1239, which inspired the connection to the Shepherd's Monument inscription. The motto surrounding the lower half of the globe was the most important element. The seven stars were a later addition.**

Accordingly, I arranged the inscription around a globe as in the Carthusian emblem, but this time fully around it, with the 'S' at the top, while keeping the lower 'D' and 'M' in the same place [see figure 23]. There still seemed to be too many 'V's and too many letters. Supposing the juxtaposed 'V' and 'A' could represent something else, something at the crux of it all? Then there would be a more logical number of 'V's left to work with. Then the words of Robert Bauval [see page 28] came back to me that the Star of David is the true sign of Jesus and embodies the fulfilment of His work!

**The 'V' and the 'A' form a Star of David when superimposed on each other**. The cross of the Carthusian emblem becomes the Star of David in the inscription because they refer to the same thing. This crux or kernel of the whole idea would go in the centre of the diagram, hence in the circle. The remaining six letters can be rotated around the circle until the 'U' is at the bottom, which then forms the 'DUM' of the emblem.

The two 'V's and two 'O's tally with the salient sounds of

# The Carthusian Connection

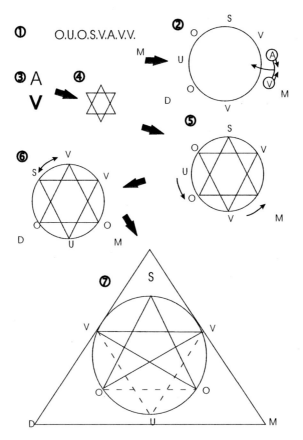

**Figure 23: The diagrammatical steps starting from the mysterious inscription on the Shepherds's Monument at Shugborough and arriving at the essence of the Carthusian emblem.**

'volvitur orbis', although the purists would say that one 'O' is missing in 'orbis'. It could be included in 'volvitur'. But I am looking for symmetry in the diagram and the two 'O's reflect that, while emphasising the globe of the diagram. To keep symmetry, I would transpose the 'S' and one 'V' so that the 'S' sits on top of the globe while the 'V's sit atop the 'O's.

In this way, the whole idea is reinforced pictorially of the world turning around the work of Jesus (Crux) represented by the Seal of Solomon/Star of David, of which the ever-constant nature is shown by the 'Stat' on top of the world.

Now the meaning was clear, but why should the Carthusians be linked in this way?

With the Star of David within the circle, it is immediately apparent that the six letters around it correspond to each point. If the 'U' is considered to be part of the lower line, forming 'DUM', then the five letters form a pentacle. This was exactly the geometry I had discovered inherent in the landscape of the Chartreuse at the start of my research in this locality. There was one other geometrical feature to add, the triangular pyramid, to take me all the way across the landscape to the Bauges and Chambéry. Surely this is why the 'DUM' line is set lower than the rest of the inscription? I drew the line and it is easy to construct a pyramid around the whole design.

Other points then struck me:

- 'S' is at the top of the design. The Carthusian emblem starts and ends with the letter 'S': 'Stat....Orbis';
- the 'DUM' part of the inscription is the middle word and accordingly sits at the base of the circular idea;
- the 'V's also represent the Chalice, the Womb, the female fertility symbol, and by extension, Marie Magdalene;
- the perpendicular from the pyramid apex would cut through the 'S' and equal the symbol for wisdom/ knowledge, ie. the serpent coiled around a staff. This would be the hidden wisdom, deliberately obscured, *within the pyramid*, or the female Holy Spirit, as represented by Mary Magdalene;
- the six-pointed star is also the coat of arms of Rennes-le-Château;
- the relief is a mirror image of the Poussin painting. A mirror image of my solution to the inscription would not produce any great difference: just the 'DUM' and 'S' reversed, but still instantly recognisable.

So the inscription at Shugborough is directly linked to the Carthusian emblem in the Chartreuse, but the question as to whose agency or influence was needed to effect this needed elucidation. The geometry of it led me through the very steps that I had taken to arrive at the Bauges and Chambéry. However, the history of the emblem was worth finding out as the next step.

# PART TWO: THE CARTHUSIAN EMBLEM

André Ravier states in the commemorative brochure for the ninth centenary of St Bruno's arrival in the Chartreuse that at the start of the Order, the fields, the books and ironwork were marked by just a simple cross. The motto and the globe, surmounted by the cross, appeared in the thirteenth century, while the stars only began to figure on seals or sculptures during the seventeenth, becoming widespread in the eighteenth century [see figure 22].

As soon as I saw that the motto and globe had been added in the thirteenth century, I realised that there might just be a possible connection between this addition and events elsewhere in southern France, namely the Albigensian Crusade against the Cathars, culminating in the fall of Montségur in 1244.

The precise answer for the date came courtesy of Aimé and his network of erudite scholars. He sent me photocopies from a book printed in Montreuil-sur-Mer (not quite from the area!) in 1891, entitled 'Sigillographie de l'Ordre des Chartreux et Numismatique de Saint Bruno' whose author was G.Vallier. This is basically a study of the Carthusian emblems and seals. From a latin account in the text, a certain highly respected prior, Domnus Martinus, was elected to highest office within the Carthusian Order when Pope Gregory IX was in power. Domnus it was who bestowed on the Order the motto and globe below the cross. This was in 1239. This was just what I had been hoping for. The 'crusade' against the heretics had begun in 1209, so this Carthusian date fell as the end was coming for the Cathars after 30 years of unrelenting genocide aginst them.

I cannot as yet prove any definite connection between the

156

two events. Yet the Templars were actively in secret consort with the Cathars. If they knew that secret documents had to be spirited away from the region and that the Cathars were most likely going to be obliterated, then a further 'signpost' in the area most likely to serve as a refuge would be very welcome. There had been collusion earlier between the two Orders of Carthusians and Templars in the matter of St Hugon and Richerenches in the 1170's, so why not at this time, when the end was inevitable for the Cathars? No doubt the House of Savoy was informed about this additional part of the emblem, as they had quite intimate ties with the Carthusians. In 1388, for example, Bonne de Bourbon, Countess of Savoy, passed an Act with them about using the emblem on marker stones to set out the extent of their property. Perhaps Domnus Martinus himself knew nothing of these machinations, but the timing is most propitious. The Order now would have an official motto to herald itself,

**Figure 24: A lesser known seal of the Carthusians, which has moved the cross within the body of the seal. The cross itself reflects the Templar emblem, especially the small one at the top.**

the Cathars' last major stronghold surrenders five years later, and those responsible for the secreting away of the precious documents would have more than just an official picture to refer to.

I could now see a clearer connection between this emblem and Shugborough.

One other seal of interest that caught my eye in the assorted notes from Vallier's book was, again, a circular one with a cross within the main body rather than around it [see figure 24]. This echoed my conclusion about putting the Star of David within the globe on the other main emblem. The cross here is highly reminiscent of the 'croix pattée' of the Templars or the Celtic cross . . . or could this just be a fixation on my part?

# PART THREE: THE SHUGBOROUGH BACKGROUND PLAYERS

**Charles Radclyffe** was the son of an illegimate daughter of the Stuart King Charles II. The Earl of Lichfield, George Lee, was also the son of one of Charles II's bastard children. So Charles Radclyffe was both cousin to 'Bonnie Prince Charlie' and the Earl of Lichfield. He became highly involved in the Jacobite Movement, when Charles II's successor, James III, was sent into exile and he tried to re-establish the Stuart throne. In 1715, there was a Jacobite rebellion, when Charles and his brother took part, were arrested and were imprisoned. Charles managed to escape with the help of his cousin, the Earl of Lichfield, fleeing to France for protection with Jacobite sympathisers.

He immediately became personal secretary to Bonnie Prince Charlie, founded the first Scottish Rite Masonic Lodge in Paris in 1725 and was the Grand Master of all French lodges for a decade. After 30 years, Bonnie Prince Charlie returned to try and retake the throne in Britain. Charles was captured and was beheaded at the Tower of London.

He had been deeply involved in freemasonry, in particular the Scottish Rite, which was claimed to descend directly from the Knights Templar and the Stuart dynasty. This version of freemasonry contained greater and more momentous secrets than later, less initiated ones, such as the 'York Rite'.

Hence the seat of the Earl of Lichfield bore witness to strong Masonic activity which had begun in the previous century. Family members provided the strongest possible link between the Templars and the Stuart dynasty through Radclyffe's French connections. When the Shugborough estate was bought by the Anson family, the status of the owners was surely a pre-requisite to the Masonic traditions being continued. Great patronage of the arts and George's elevated position in the Navy would have ensured that in an elitist society.

Radclyffe had been at the head of the French lodges and of the alleged Priory of Sion, so his connections with the Templars and his knowledge of their covert beliefs and operations were assured. The Earls of Lichfield had family links to the Stuarts. What struck me as extraordinary here was the categoric assertion by the Royal Stuart Society that the direct and legitimate male line of the Royal House of Stuart ended in 1807, whereafter **its Headship passed to the House of Savoy** by virtue of its descent from Henrietta-Anne (1644–1670), daughter of King Charles I, and her husband, Philippe, Duke of Orléans [see page 59]. The House of Savoy was based in Chambéry. The fact that the Templars and the House of Savoy had enjoyed close common interests for centuries was now borne out through the Stuarts who would not have ceded their dynastic rights simply by a process akin to sticking a pin in a list! They would have been very aware of the House of Savoy's pedigree and of their connections with the Carthusians.

The link between Shugborough and the Carthusians was not looking so bizarre now.

**Thomas Wright** (1711–1786) was the first architect involved with the monuments. During the six years of his work for Thomas Anson, he had attributed to him parts of the Ruin and the Shepherd's Monument. He was a celebrated astronomer, architect, antiquary and mathematician with an interest in the occult. The Information Department at Shugborough could not verify definitely whether he had had Masonic leanings or not, but the possibility, I was told, seems heavily weighted to the probable.

**James 'Athenian' Stuart** (1713–1788) was an architect,

archeologist and painter who had a hand in the completion of the Shepherd's Monument. He was responsible for the classical Greek monuments whose style he actively researched in Athens in the company of Nicholas Revett. Would it be too much of an assumption to say that he had family links to the Stuart dynasty and therefore had links with the Masons? Shugborough could not say definitely.

# PART FOUR: THE POUSSIN PAINTING

From the above indications and links, it would appear that the Poussin painting copied on the Shugborough Shepherd's Monument should be linked as well with the Chartreuse and Chambéry area, to reinforce the solution of the inscription decoding. 'Les Bergers d'Arcadie' [see figure 25] has been studied by Henry Lincoln in minute detail [see select bibliography] and he made a strong case with a spot near Arques and the Lawrence family tomb which he equates with the one in the painting. The immediate background mountain outline behind the tomb is not a complete fit with the location near Rennes, but that on the far right of the picture is highly reminiscent.

In c.1640, Poussin made the trip from Rome to Paris, but his actual route is not known, an acknowledgement that Lincoln eventually managed to force from the art historians. He concludes that Poussin made a detour to Rennes or possibly worked from sketches. It would certainly have needed to be a strong motivation to go to such lengths, as the detour is not a small one. The tomb near Arques did not apparently contain anything of great historical note and has been razed by the owners to prevent any further desecration by treasure hunters.

My hypothesis is that Poussin did not have to make a lengthy detour because Chambéry is practically on the way from Rome to Paris. Via either Grenoble or up the Rhône valley from Lyon, there is little extra journey to make, if at all, compared to the Languedoc. If he had wanted to make a statement about the Cathar treasure, then the seat of the House of Savoy at Chambéry makes a perfect staging-post.

The main reason for placing the painting in or near Chambéry is the cliff promontory right above the tomb. This is a near-perfect replica of Mt Nivolet, with the sloping ridge

162

**Figure 25: 'The Shepherds of Arcadia' by Nicolas Poussin. The salient outcrop appears directly behind the tomb. The sloping ridge down to the left closely follows that of Mt Nivolet down past Pragondran and le Sire. To avoid making the actual pinnacle too obviously detectable, I believe Poussin painted it in mirror image, which then fits the outline of the present mountain top almost exactly. This clue is inherent in the mirror image of the Shepherd's Monument at Shugborough.**

to the left above Pragondran. Yet just the pinnacle outline itself seems back to front. *The mirror image of the Shugborough copy suddenly assumed great relevance*, as this would be a simple and effective way of disguising the identity of the site. The test in a mirror proved conclusive, as the match is practically complete, taking into account the passing of three and a half centuries. The vantage point would appear to be in the axis of the Chapelle St Saturnin as opposed to the Crypt of Lémenc or the château which are both slightly to the right (east), but both of the latter are in practically the same line. The Chapelle St Saturnin is about halfway on the nearest road link between the two hamlets of Sonnaz and Pragondran, which lie beneath the two chambers of the pyramid. In its way, it would seem quite a fitting spot to place the painting.

The church of St Pierre-de-Lémenc stands on the ancient remains of a temple dedicated to Mercury from Roman times. Lémenc is mentioned from the year 50AD. It was a Roman staging post on the imperial route from Milan to Lyon. It stands above the present city centre to the north, nestling underneath Mt Nivolet, although the direct view is obscured by the growth of building over the years. This was the main route through the valley at that time as the valley floor was very marshy, the result of the lac du Bourget being longer than it is today. Built at the end of the fifteenth century, using the walls of the previous Romanesque church which burnt down in 1445, it contains some ancient tombs, including that of St Concord, the Irish Archbishop who died at Lémenc in 1176. But the most surprising news for myself, when I researched further, was that a venerable Black Virgin dominates the eastern part of the lower structure [see plate 28]. This reinforced my suspicions of connections between this area and the Isis–Mary Magdalene link, especially with the Black Virgin figuring so prominently at Myans.

**Plate 28: The crypt of Lémenc. The Black Virgin stands in the back corner. The large tomb represents Jesus with attendant disciples and women after the Crucifixion. It was badly damaged during the Revolution.**

The château provides another perfect viewpoint of Mt Nivolet. This was the stronghold of the House of Savoy, obtained in 1295 by Count Amédée V, whose grandfather, Thomas I, had acquired the town in 1232. The town had been building up over two centuries at the foot of the château.

The Sainte Chapelle in the château had been the home of the Holy Shroud from 1502 until 1578, minus a period when it was withdrawn for security reasons to stay with the House of Savoy between 1536 and 1561. Then a temporary transfer to Turin became permanent. So there was a gap of about 60 years before Poussin would have passed through here. This good view of Mt Nivolet would be from right next to the Sainte Chapelle. Another very famous 'tomb', indeed, to inspire a painting?

This famous painting by Poussin highlights Mt Nivolet from the front, the south/south-west.

The 'Et in Arcadia Ego' motif appears also in an earlier painting by him, dating from either 1630 or 1635, where the tomb is surmounted by a skull and, crucially, is **sited in the side of a cliff** [figure 26]. My conclusion is that this represents the cliff above Pragondran, as highlighted by the cross-shaped phenomenon. To reinforce this is the bearded water-deity in the foreground of the painting, the river god, Alpheus, lord of the underground stream. My research into the speleology of this massif leapt back into focus with its kilometres of underground systems. Indeed, just around the headland is le trou de la Doriaz and la grotte Carret, where the river gushes out of the cliff in spectacular fashion and rushes down towards Chambéry. Poussin could well have represented the more exact location in this earlier painting and then given the general location in the more famous one, by showing Mt Nivolet right behind the tomb.

But for many, the question must remain: why should this painting be rated so highly and seem so mysterious?

Poussin had been linked repeatedly with the Saunière story at Rennes-le-Château. He had been visited in Rome in 1656 by the Abbé Louis Fouquet, brother of Nicholas Fouquet, Superintendent of Finances to Louis XIV of France. A letter sent to Nicholas by Louis Fouquet described his meeting with Poussin and stated that some great secret

**Figure 26: The earlier painting on the same theme by Poussin, which locates the tomb in the side of a cliff. I believe this equates to the cliffs above Pragondran. Alpheus, the god of the underground stream, highlights the locality, which has extensive underground networks. He is here reclining on the ground. The only mountain outline visible, in the middle left-hand side, is cut by the shepherdess's robe in such a way that Mt Granier is pictured in detail, with the section left after the 1248 collapse clearly discernible.**

would be told him on his return which could remain beyond the reach even of kings and would possibly remain hidden in the centuries to come.

Nicholas Fouquet was soon arrested and imprisoned for the rest of his life. Louis XIV went to great pains to monitor all of Fouquet's correspondence and obtained the original painting of 'les Bergers d'Arcadie' so that he could examine it in private. The belief that the painting held some encoded secret for the initiated has not lost its attraction over the centuries.

# PART FIVE: OTHER CLUES AT SHUGBOROUGH

The **Ruin** [see figure 27] came immediately to my attention, as previously mentioned, because of its elements which have strong echoes of my mountainous geometry around Chambéry. As very little now remains [see plates 29 and 30] – only part of the Druid on the mound of rubble – I have taken as my reference the picture by Nicholas Dall from 1775:

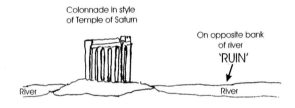

Colonnade in style
of Temple of Saturn

On opposite bank
of river
'RUIN'

River

River

THE 'RUIN'

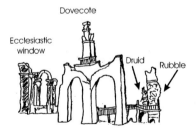

Dovecote

Ecclesiastic
window

Druid

Rubble

**Figure 27: The Colonnade (destroyed by flood about 200 years ago) at Shugborough based on the Temple of Saturn at Rome. On the opposite bank of the river, the 'Ruin', comprising the three basic elements of the pyramid in the research.**

167

**Plate 29: The Ruin at Shugborough. This all that remains – part of a balustrade, the mound of rubble and part of a Druid figure halfway up on the left.**

- the Gothic dovecote, which was most probably ornamental in its conception before being used practically, (according to the Information Dept. at Shugborough), is the English representation and translation of *le Colombier,* the mountain at the apex of the pyramid. It towers in the middle above the two other items at either end;
- at one corner at the base of the pyramid is Mt Granier, of which a part collapsed in 1248, killing about 5000 people and obliterating villages. At one end of the Ruin, the Druid sits on a rubble crag. This could well represent the rubble left from the collapse, rubble which is all too apparent even today around Apremont at the base of Mt Granier;
- I had postulated that the Celtic era had been at the forefront of the establishment of the huge geometry in the Chartreuse. The Druid would represent this;
- at the other end of the Ruin is only what could be described as the vaulted remnant of an ecclesiastical

**Plate 30: The Druid and rubble. Part of the Druid is missing.**

doorway or window. Interestingly, fragments of the former palace of the Bishops of Lichfield were used in the building of the Ruin. The other corner of the pyramid in Savoy is Hautecombe Abbey.

So the three points of interest of the Ruin, which seem entirely incongruous, unconnected, or even haphazard, suddenly become meaningful representations of three points of the pyramid. Looking at them from the river side, in which case the dovecote would be slightly removed to the rear and thus in the correct position as represented by le Colombier on the map, the two end items would appear to be reversed. Yet, the clue to the configuration, the mirror image (as already portrayed by the Poussin painting on the Shepherd's Monument), taken from behind the dovecote on the garden side, would 'correct' this anomaly. I can only assume that this was done to veil the significance of the Ruin.

Opposite the Ruin, on the bank of the river, there stood a classical **colonnade** [see figure 27], which, according to the guidebook, was possibly an adaptation of the *Temple of Saturn* in the Roman Forum. This rather strange architecture, erected at Wright's instigation, disappeared probably at the time of the Great Flood in 1795. The view of Mt Nivolet which seems most likely from the Poussin painting is in the axis of the cleft or gorge in the hill where the *Chapelle St Saturnin* is situated. Could this coincidence of name be purely fortuitous?

The old route or path at the foot of this gorge was very important at the time when the plain below in the Chambéry valley was still invaded by water and marshland as a result of the longer reach of the lac du Bourget to the south-east. It is known that the 'Via Saturnina', a branch of the main Roman route from Milan to Vienne, passed through this gorge on its way to Aix-les-Bains and Geneva.

The chapel of St Saturnin [see plate 31] seems to have its roots in the first centuries of Christendom. According to

**Plate 31: The St Saturnin chapel. Set back from the road, it is partly esconced in the cliff wall.**

**Plate 32: The chapel interior. A large tomb behind which can be seen the bare rock of the rear wall.**

legend, in this same spot was a cave or were temple ruins dedicated to Saturn. In about 245AD, St Saturnin, sent by the Pope to convert heretics and pagans, arrived in this gorge, overturned the idol of the false god, and caused a miraculous fountain to gush out of the rock. One hypothesis put forward by archeologists is that the site was a sepulchral cave [see plate 32] and that the chapel was constructed in honour of St Saturnin some time after his martyrdom as Bishop in Toulouse in the mid-third century. However, there does not appear to be any documentary proof of the saint's visit to the region nor any authentic mention of the legend. The first mention of any cult celebrated on this spot is in 1340.

The chapel's upkeep depends on the commune of Vérel-Pragondran, whose parish priest in 1839, Barthélemy Perrier, wrote a note to a poem in praise of the chapel, according to which relics of St Saturnin remained in it, but without giving any clues to their origin. Some measure of authenticity seems to have been shown by the great veneration accorded to this chapel by Mgr Martinet, the Archbishop of Chambéry between 1828 and 1839, who contributed generously to its restoration in 1839 and granted an annual subsidy for its maintenance. I am indebted for my notes here to extracts from Philibert Falcoz *La Gorge de St Saturnin*.

The chapel now is quite well maintained, which, even so, belies its rather more exalted past. Poussin could very well have chosen this spot on his way through towards Paris as the viewpoint for his painting.

One other monument in the gardens with an oblique echo of the Chambéry area is the **Cat's Monument** [see plate 33]. It faces the Shepherd's Monument across the river, but the growth of the trees has blocked the view. Oddly enough,

**Plate 33: The Cat's Monument. The cat is perched right on the top. Other vague echoes of the Carthusian emblem are the large globe of the vase/urn and the semi-circular shape of the wreath below it.**

172

**Plate 34: The fireplace in the Shugborough Dining Room. The original place reserved for the Shepherd's Monument elements could well have been here, in place of the portrait of Admiral Lord Anson. The lower surround contains floral designs appertaining to Bacchus.**

across the southern end of the lac du Bourget facing Mt Nivolet is a distinctive peak jutting up above the parallel ridge of the last Jura spur, called *la Dent du Chat*, or the *Cat's Tooth*.

In the House, the **Dining Room** was brought to my attention. A possible original siting for the Shepherd's Monument could have been here above the fireplace (a personal view of my contact at Shugborough, which is also more widely accepted by the staff) [see plate 34]. The guidebook does state in similar vein that the monument was originally conceived in wood as shown by the unusual swirling carving on the curved arch and to be 'the more retired the better, as in a Saloon or Lawnet, being chiefly designed for the Enjoyment of Objects near the eye'.

The **medallion heads** in the cove are unusual in that they represent the Egyptian deities, Isis on the left of the room and Osiris (Serapis) on the right, with Dionysus/ Bacchus directly above the fireplace. The guidebook says that this is a strange choice which again suggests that Thomas Wright, with his interest in astronomy and the occult, was responsible for the general decorative scheme. The marble chimney-piece has a Bacchic mask and garlands of vines. My interest is due to the following reasons:

- Isis, and her goddess cult, is the precursor of the Black Virgins phenomenon. There are Black Virgins at St Pierre de Lémenc and at Myans, both very historic sites in the immediate vicinity of Chambéry;
- Osiris is the original pharaoh god, the consort of Isis. As such, le Sire would be an aptly derived title through both the spelling and meaning and is the name of the place situated above the northern end of the cliffs above Pragondran;
- Bacchus reflects the Gorges de Bacchus on the right of the cliffs above Pragondran.

These heads are in the Dining Room on either side of, and above, the fireplace; in other words, as a complement to the message which would have been inherent in the marble relief, had it been positioned there (as probably originally intended) and not outside.

One thing struck me at first as odd, if all this elaborate arrangement was carefully and deliberately plotted to give salient clues. Why were Isis and Osiris on opposite sides, if the view from Pragondran was to be adhered to? Then the mirror image process came back to me. In that case, Osiris (le Sire) would be to the left and Isis (Black Virgin) to the right. Then that fitted the immediate geography of the Pragondran vicinity.

I now added the Shugborough side of the equation to the 'flow-chart' in figure 28 page 136.

I feel confident that all these clues at Shugborough, not

just the inscription itself on the Shepherd's Monument, point back towards the repository of some momentous secret stashed away in the headland overlooking Chambéry. I cannot state with any certainty what might be found, but there has been intense speculation about what the Templars and the Cathars might have possessed in the way of heretical artefacts or documents and what pains they took to protect and hide them.

The 'route' I have taken through my research did not start with the major historical landmarks of the area. From Mt St Michel south to the Chartreuse; then back north to hamlets highlighted by geometry near Chambéry; finally back to the major famous sites within the city itself. This circuitous or roundabout trail from minor to major reinforces the idea that it was a real journey of discovery I embarked upon over a decade ago. There were no pre-planned discoveries or travel directions. One finding followed another, almost as if I was being gently led in a circle. Obvious famous sites had been bypassed earlier in my research, only to re-appear as important later on. The most salient point overlooking Chambéry directly is Mt Nivolet. It is hardly surprising then that I was led all around it before 'landing' on it at the conclusion.

# ADDENDA AND POSTSCRIPT

## *Addendum: 1. From Mt St Michel*

As an experiment, I extended the fan-like 15° system of alignments that had led me from Mt St Michel to Chamechaude in the transitional stage from the Chambéry valley to the Chartreuse. Again, this threw up some interesting points:

- the next line 15° west from the 'baseline': it passes within 75m. of the summit of la Pointe de la Bornée;
- the next line in the series: it passes within the same distance of the col du Planet;
- the next: this one passes through the church at Challes-les-Eaux, a cross by the road at le Mapas, before leading back to Mt Grelle at the intersection of the line north from Chamechaude and the east-west line through Myans;
- at 30° further west: this line leads to Chambéry Cathedral through the church at la Ravoire on its hill;
- at 15° to the north-west: it passes through three châteaux – Bressieux, Caramagne, and Servolex;
- a further 15° north-west: it aligns the château of St Alban with the col between le Molard noir and la Dent du Chat;
- at 30° round from the line to les Marches in the south-east: this line hits la Savoyarde/le Roc de Torméry ie. it meets the line going east-west from Mt Grelle through Myans to la Roche du Guet.

All these points reinforce the effect of the panoramic view from the chapel on Mt St Michel and my conviction that the earliest builders of churches and other landmarks in the area put it to good use as surveyors.

177

### Addendum: 2. 'Saint' Louis?

Louis was born in 1214 whereas St Bernard died in 1153. But Greg Rigby states: 'the influence of the Cistercians in the early part of the thirteenth century must have been pervasive and it may well be that a "Holy" king would have been party to secrets which were previously kept from others'. In 1257, 'Saint' Louis assisted in the consecration of the choir of the Cathedral of St Quentin. It could be argued that he had a part in the knowledge of the groundplan of the Plough, hence his gift of the Black Madonna to the Carthusians provides a link in addition to the connection between St Robert and St Bruno.

It is strange how he returns to the investigation as the persecutor of the Cathars alongside his relations with Béatrice of Savoy and his part in her loss of status.

### Addendum: 3. The Golden Section

This relates to a line being divided to provide a particular proportion: the lesser part is to the greater as the greater is to the whole: the line AC below is divided at B so that AB is to BC as BC is to AC [not to scale here]. Expressed mathematically, the proportion is 1 : 1.618

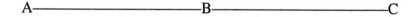

A————————————————B————————————————C

The pentacle is a Golden Section figure. The chords intersect each other in this same ratio.

This proportion was recognised in antiquity as an intrinsic part of sacred geometry and was used extensively, for example, in the building of medieval Gothic cathedrals.

# FINAL THOUGHTS

The foundation of the Carthusian Order dates back for more than 900 years. Innumerable studies have been made on the subject. After the ten or so years of wondering about and searching for the basic geometry of the natural 'temple' on the map, plus all the walks and on-the-spot research, I feel now that I can say with some confidence that this investigation presents, firstly, a completely different perspective on the founding of Myans and the Chartreux Order, as described in the first section of this work.

The conclusions of the second section are contentious, but the weight of circumstantial evidence, based on both history and local evidence, is difficult to refute, along with the geometry which fits the landscape. I realise that I cannot prove conclusively my assertions. There remains much further investigation to be done: to enquire at greater length into the history of the House of Savoy, to pinpoint further historical references to confirm the geometric findings on the map, and further local fieldwork. If it opens up a new area of study on the region, then so much the better.

The final section has been an eye-opener for me as I had no idea that Shugborough would even come into the reckoning. The realisation of its importance as some kind of confirmatory evidence really only came after all the rest of the manuscript had been prepared. Yet I cannot help wondering why Thomas Wright and, especially, James Stuart would have bothered with all the seemingly extraneous monuments, if they knew all about the meaning of those that pertain to France and which would have stood out in importance. Presumably, livelihoods had to be earned by following the fashions of the day and the whims of those less initiated than themselves.

It seems odd, nevertheless, that the geometry and the linked collusions behind the scenes between the main protagonists have not surfaced before, at least not in the public domain. Have the Carthusians, the Cistercians and the House of Savoy, along with the Templars, had more knowledge than they are prepared to admit or has this 'secret' history been lost over time? There might well have been breaks in the transmission of it, through such things as natural disasters – such as the collapse of the cardinal point of Mt Granier – untimely deaths, even persecution/'heretical cleansing' or decisions made about site placements without real explanations. But there is one constant which has always been highlighted throughout history, namely that information enshrined in art, stone and mathematics has lasted and will remain the longest time, even covertly. One has only to consider the wealth of information still coming from the Pyramids, even after all that is encoded within its dimensions has been analysed. We still cannot fully explain how or when they were built nor for what purpose exactly without heated polemic. While this research is not remotely on the same scale, a tremendous effort was made to construct sacred geometry in the landscape, involving many people over a great time period. The work is not yet complete.

# SELECT BIBLIOGRAPHY AND REFERENCES

Baigent L, Leigh R, Lincoln H (1982) *The Holy Blood and the Holy Grail* Corgi

Lincoln H (1997) *Key to the Sacred Pattern* Windrush Press

Markale J (2003) *Montségur and the Mystery of the Cathars* Inner Traditions, Rochester, Vermont. Translated by J Graham from original (2001) *Montségur et l'énigme cathare* Pygmalion, Paris.

Begg E (1985) *The Cult of the Black Virgin* Penguin/Arkana, London.

Guides Gallimard (1998) *France Isère* Editions Nouveaux Loisirs

Guides Gallimard (1998) *France Médiévale* Editions du Patrimoine

Krikorian J-C (1984) *St Bruno et les Chartreux. La Tradition Vivante* Editions C.I.F. Pères de Notre-Dame de Myans, *Notre Dame de Myans* Lescuyer, Lyons.

Spillemaecker C (1996) *La Grande Chartreuse: le désert et les hommes* Editions Le Dauphiné

Wood D (1985) *Genisis* Baton Press

Wood D, Campbell I (1994) *Geneset* Belleme Books

Doumergue C (2001) *L'Evangile Interdit – Ste Marie Madeleine et le secret des Cathares* C Lacour (ed.)

**Maps:**
IGN Top 25 [1:25 000]
Richard D *Randonnée Pédestre et à ski* [Series 1:50 000]

**Page 5**
Baigent L, Leigh R, Lincoln H (1982) *op cit*

# Select Bibliography and References

**Page 6**

Pachoud A (1983) *Notre-Dame de Myans* Montmélian

**Page 11**

Nicholson H J Lecture to Saunière Society 4 October 2003 – based on her book *The Knights Templar: A New History* (2001) Sutton

**Page 16**

Picknett L, Price C (1997) *The Templar Revelation* Bantam

Armengaud M (1992) *Orcival* Autoédition

Cassagnes-Brouquet S (2000) *Vierges Noires* Rouergues, Rodez

Picknett L (2003) *Mary Magdalene* Robinson, London

**Page 17**

Bonvin J *Vierges Noires – La réponse vient de la terre* Dervy, Paris

**Page 20**

Berlioz J (1998) *L'Effrondrement du Mt Granier en Savoie (1248)* C.A.R.E., Musée Dauphinois, Grenoble

**Page 28**

Vialate A (1995) *Légendes (des Montagnes) Vertigineuses du Dauphiné* Editions Christian de Bertillat

le Bras G (1979) *Les Ordres Religieux – la vie et l'art* Tome 1, Flammarion

**Page 29**

(1950) *La Grande Chartreuse par un Chartreux* (9th edition) Porthand

A Côte (1882) *La Grande Chartreuse par un Chartreux* (2nd edition)– libraire – Editeur Grenoble

Thompson E M (1930) *The Carthusian Order in England* SPCK, Church Historical Society, London

Pascal M A (1868) *Le désert de la Grande Chartreuse* Maison Ville et Fils, Grenoble

**Page 33**

*Encyclopédie d'Aujourdhui* Edition Livre de Poche

Rigby G (1996) *On Earth as it is in Heaven* Rhaedus Publications

**Page 34**

Mitchell J (1998) *The Dimensions of Paradise* Thames & Hudson, London

Hall M P (1998) *The Secret Teachings of all Ages* Philosophical Research Society, Los Angeles
**Page 35**
Billet J (1987) *Le Guide de la Chartreuse* la Manufacture
**Page 39**
Bauval R (1999) *Secret Chamber* Century, London
Knight C, Lomas R (1996) *The Hiram Key* Century, London
**Page 50**
Ravier A (1981) *St Bruno le Chartreux* Editions P Lethielleux
 – Dessain et Tolra, Paris
**Page 51**
Thompson E M ( 1930) *op cit*
**Page 52**
Bligny B (1984) *St Bruno, le premier Chartreux* Ouest France
Löbbel H, Lefèvre Abbé *St Bruno et l'Ordre des Chartreux*
**Page 52**
Bouchayer A (1927) *Les Chartreux, Maîtres de Forge*
Côte A (1882) *op cit*
**Page 53**
Pascal M A (1868) *op cit*
Dubois M *La Grande Chartreuse: l'art religieux au monastére* Grenoble
du Boys A (1845) *La Grande Chartreuse*
**Page 54**
Gaussin P-R (1981) *Le Rayonnement de la Chaise-Dieu* Editions Watel-Brioude
**Page 57**
Rigby G (1996) *op cit*
**Page 81**
Secret Abbé B (1939) *Le Mont Revard* Librairie Dardel, Chambéry
**Page 83**
*Les Grands Mystères de l'Histoire* No 3, October 2002
**Page 86**
le Bras G (1979) *op cit*
**Page 87**
Douzet A (2001) *Saunière's Model and the Secret of Rennes-le-Château* Adventures Unlimited Press/Société Perillos

# Select Bibliography and References

**Page 88**
Baigent L, Leigh R, Lincoln H (1982) *op cit*
**Page 91**
Furlong D (1997) *The Keys to the Temple: unravel the mysteries of the Ancient World* Piatkus, London
**Page 95**
*Les Grands Mystères de l'Histoire – L'Hérésie Cathare (hors-série)* July 2003
**Page 104**
Knight C, Lomas R (1997) *The Second Messiah* Century, London
**Page 114**
Knight C, Lomas R (1996) *op cit*
**Page 121**
Picknett L (2003) op cit
Elkington D 'The Tomb of Isiris' in *Journal of Research Into Lost Knowledge Organisation*, Autumn 2003
**Page 123**
Guichenon *Histoire de la Royale Maison de Savoie* Tome I
**Page 125**
Read P P (2001) *The Templars* Phoenix Press
**Page 126**
*Templarium* DAEG, 84360 Lauris/Dervy, Paris
**Page 128**
Picknett L (2003) *op cit*
**Page 129**
*L'Hérésie Cathare* (July 2003) *op cit*
**Page 132**
www.jeanmichel.rouand.free.fr
www.terres-cathares.com
www.histoire.medievale.free.fr
Sumption J (1978) *The Albigensian Crusade* Faber & Faber, London
**Page 151**
Professor Cornford in Lincoln H (1997) *op cit* pp108–111
**Page 172**
Falcoz P (1914) *La Gorge de St Saturnin* Librairie Perrin, Imprimerie Général Savoisienne

# Index

# Index

186

# Index

Printed in the United Kingdom
by Lightning Source UK Ltd.
108557UKS00001B/188